The Warrior Anointing,

destiny awaits

Volume One

Awakening Laymen

Alan B. Keyte

Copyright @ 2012 by Alan B. Keyte

All rights reserved.

ISBN: 1468094696
ISBN-13: 978-1468094695

Library of Congress Control Number: 2012905458
CreateSpace, North Charleston, SC

Unless otherwise indicated, Bible quotations are taken from the King James Version of the Holy Bible.

Originally published as the *Authorized Version* in 1611. This edition of the KJV conforms to the text of the King James Bible printed by Cambridge University Press, from c.1900 to c.1980.

Cover Image licensed by Depositphotos.com/Igor Goncharenko.

Please note that my writing style capitalizes certain pronouns in Scripture that refer to the Father, Son and Holy Spirit, and that may differ from other writer's and publisher's styles. Also, please note that the name satan and related names are not capitalized as I choose not to acknowledge him even if it does violate grammatical rules.

Dedication

This book is dedicated to my wife, Peggy Joice Keyte; my seven children: Anthony, Donald, Haley, Adrian, Tristan, Cassie and Samantha; to my parents; my grandchildren and my great grandchildren. The Lord has indeed blessed and enriched my life beyond measure. My quiver is full and I am highly and deeply favored by the Lord Most High.

I also dedicate this book to the brave and heroic men of the Full Gospel Business Men's Fellowship, International who have blessed me with their brotherly love, generosity, wisdom and passion for Jesus, the Holy Spirit and Father God.

And, most especially I dedicate this book to the Lord Jesus, The Holy Anointed One of Israel who is both the Lamb of God and the Lion of Judah, to the precious Holy Spirit who is so vital to us in these last days and to Father God, Abba, Daddy who is more amazing than we can ever begin to imagine!

Table of Contents

Introduction..1
Assumptions...6
A Call to Arms...13
    Why Now?..23
    The Call of God..31
    Courage..38
    Life – is about People...43
    Virtue..50
The Anointing...54
    What is the Anointing?..55
    Understanding the Anointing..61
    Corporate Anointing...68
    Communion with the Holy Spirit...................................73
    The Flow of the Holy Spirit..78
    The River of Life..84
Warrior Anointing..88
Prepare for Battle...98
    Who is Our Enemy?...101
        What Does the Enemy Look Like?......................103
        Snares of the Enemy..107
    Who is God to You?...111
    Who Am I to God?...115
    Dunamis Power...118
        The Spirit with Us..122
        The Spirit in Us..124
        The Spirit upon Us...126
    Dead to Sin..129
        Antidote to the Lies...136
        Help Me! I have Fallen...139
        Walking in the Spirit...141
    Time Daily with Jesus..144
        1st Priority - Jesus Time...144
        2nd Priority - The Word..146
        3rd Priority – Prayer..149

  4th Priority – Journaling 160
  Hearing God 163
  Loving Our Neighbor 168
  Accountability partners 172
Keys to Success 177
  Accepted 179
  Commitment 182
  Consistency 185
  Obedience 186
  No Compromise 189
  Bless Others 191
  Faith and Hope 195
  Favor of the Most High 197
  Watch Your Vows 199
  Be a Voice, not an Echo 202
  Stepping Out 207
  Rules for the Road 210
  Wait upon the Lord 215
What's Next? 218
Appendixes 222
  Appendix A – The Vision 223
  Appendix B – Daily Affirmations 225
  Appendix C – Impartation of the Warrior Anointing 228
  Appendix D - Roman Road to Salvation 229
  Appendix E - Recommended Reading 230
End notes 231
Glossary 234

Acknowledgements

I would like to thank several people for their support and efforts in helping me bring this work to fruition. Foremost among them is my wife, Peggy Joice Keyte who endured long hours of separation, who listened to me and helped me refine my ideas, gave me new insight into many areas and encouraged me to continue and to persevere. She is the rock of our family and so much more pragmatic than I am. I love, cherish and adore her for her support and her love.

Then, I am so grateful to Alan Koeneman and Gerald Loper, both from the Tucson chapter of the Full Gospel Business Men's Fellowship International, for their immeasurable help in the editing and review process of this book and I will be forever grateful for your friendship, support, ideas and love. I am also grateful to John Carrette, International Executive Vice President for the United States of America, of the Full Gospel Business Men's Fellowship International, who provided much inspiration and fodder for this work. And, I am thankful for Pastor Robert Choate, of City Talks and Christ Comfort Ministries International, and Darci Schreiber for their support and assistance with ideas, publication contacts and encouragement. You are all my dear friends and I love you very much indeed.

Finally, I thank and praise God for His inspiration, guidance and wisdom in helping me accomplish this work. Truly, without His help and inspiration this would not have happened as He has been preparing me all my life for the days just ahead of us. Praise God for His wonderful work among men!

Introduction

Ephesians 6:12 For we wrestle not against flesh and blood, but against principalities, against powers, against the rulers of the darkness of this world, against spiritual wickedness in high *places.*

"Too long have we been waiting for one another to begin! The time of waiting is past! The hour of God has struck! War is declared! In God's Holy Name let us arise and build! 'The God of Heaven, He will fight for us', as we for Him. We will not build on the sand, but on the bedrock of the sayings of Christ, and the gates and minions of hell shall not prevail against us. Should such men as we fear? Before the world, yes, before the sleepy, lukewarm, faithless, namby-pamby Christian world, we will dare to trust our God, we will venture our all for Him, we will live and we will die for Him, and we will do it with His joy unspeakable singing aloud in our hearts..." ~ CT Studd

"God has shown me the future, and has revealed that 'A New Wave of Revival' is about to EXPLODE within the body of Christ. A new wave of revival, a new wave of repentance, a new wave of holiness and a mighty outpouring of the Holy Spirit power ..." ~ Bernard Njotorahardjo, National President - FGBMFI Indonesia.

The Warrior Anointing, destiny awaits

When I first envisioned *The Warrior Anointing*, I saw a warrior in armor with his head bowed kneeling before the Lord Jesus to receive the anointing and the power he needed for the journey ahead. Beneath the armor, the warrior was drenched with sweat and blood, and he was shaking with exhaustion from the exertion of his trial thus far. His arms hung limp at his sides and he had the appearance of one who was thoroughly spent.

That sounds like a description of many Christians I know who struggle with unseen forces bent on their destruction. *The Warrior Anointing* as a phrase cannot be found in scripture, but the idea of being or becoming a warrior for Jesus is certainly found all throughout scripture. This series of books will illustrate what it really takes to become a true warrior for the Lord, how to discern the enemies activities, how to seek him out and then how to destroy his works.

1 John 3:8 … For this purpose the Son of God was manifested, that he might destroy the works of the devil.

Most people envision the idea of a warrior as someone who trains and engages in physical combat. Even the word warrior invokes images of physical combat. Yet, being a warrior for Jesus is not about the physical aspects of warfare even though at times it might feel like you have been in a physical battle. But, as a spiritual warrior, most of our battles will be fought on our knees as we pray and intercede for people, communities and nations. We do not overcome evil by meeting it head on with greater force, or by returning blow for blow or evil for evil. We overcome evil and the evil one with good; by doing good, or the right thing in every situation that arises. We overcome evil with truth. We do not overcome evil in our own strength, but in the strength and anointing bestowed upon us by God. Power, love and a sound mind are key instruments in this war and these are our principle weapons.

Introduction

2 Timothy 1:7 For God hath not given us the spirit of fear; but of power, and of love, and of a sound mind.

For most of my adult life, I have been aware of the nearness of the *"end of days."* I am very aware that time is limited and we are approaching the end. I was first made aware of the nearness of the end during the 1973 Arab-Israeli war. Even though I was unsaved at that time, I possessed an awareness of God's presence and His holiness that still seems incredible to me now. I had just finished reading *The Late Great Planet Earth*, by Hal Lindsey and I knew then that I was watching history being made, and that the bible was being fulfilled right before my eyes. My friends, the hour is late and we need to be about our Father's business, just as Jesus told His parents when he was twelve years old:

Luke 2:49 And he said unto them, How is it that ye sought me? wist ye not that I must be about my Father's business?

And this perception that we are on the edge of eternity has only grown more imperative and more intense over the years. We see scripture being fulfilled nearly on a daily basis as the world and current events race to meet their maker. I have an alarm sounding in my head most of the time. When I watch the news which is not as often as it used to be, I am awestruck with how close we are to the end of all things and the start of the reign of our God and Savior.

We, the ordinary, day to day people of God, must prepare for war, seek out the enemy and destroy all his works! We need to be about the Lord's work when our Lord and Savior returns – not just sitting around and waiting for Him to rescue us. He did not tell us go somewhere and hide. He told us to tell everyone, really everything that draws breath that He is the son of God, that He paid our price for us, that He can and will save us, and that he is coming back to claim us. That has been His message to His church ever since He went home to sit at the right hand of the Father. Jesus is not coming for a grey dingy church, but for a white church. One that is pure and holy.

Mark 16:15 And he said unto them, Go ye into all the world, and preach the gospel to every creature.

This work, this book, is the work of the Lord. As I said earlier, the Lord has been preparing me all my life for the days just ahead. The awesome days of the last great revival are almost upon us. The souls of men hang in the balance and the fields are white – ripe and ready for harvest.

John 4:35 Say not ye, There are yet four months, and *then* cometh harvest? behold, I say unto you, Lift up your eyes, and look on the fields; for they are white already to harvest.

This book teaches men how to prepare to become valiant warriors, how to discern the activity of the enemy and then how to seek him out and destroy his works. It really is that simple and straightforward. God has called us and equipped us; all we have to do is answer the call. We get to choose whether or not we will participate in the greatest adventure and the greatest battle of all time! We need to awaken our brothers, our fellow laymen to the challenge and ensure they too are prepared for the days ahead.

This call is not to professional laity, to the clergy, but to ordinary laymen. This is for every single person who loves God and will obey Him no matter what. The Warrior Anointing is the anointing that fulfills the following verse and breaks the yoke off of God's people everywhere:

Isaiah 10:27 And it shall come to pass in that day, *that* his burden shall be taken away from off thy shoulder, and his yoke from off thy neck, and the yoke shall be destroyed because of the anointing.

This is the Lord's clarion call to all who have ears to hear:

> Wake Up My People! Arise!
> Arise Mighty Warriors!
> Arise, Valiant Ones!

Take Your Places and Stand!
Receive the Warrior Anointing,
Destiny Awaits!

As I said earlier, this is all God's doing – His thoughts and ideas, His work. So, to the Lord be all the glory, honor and praise forever more! I am just trying to convey His message.

Father, I pray that everyone who is reading this is blessed by the audacity and simplicity of your message and your plan. I pray that it heightens their awareness of the changes needed to bring them into agreement with you and your ways, and that it changes their lives in such a way that they will never, never ever be the same again! In the matchless name of Jesus, the Anointed One! Amen

Assumptions

"What can render the state of a person worse than to be an enemy of God, Jesus Christ, and the power of godliness; and yet to think he is holy and a good Christian?" ~ Benjamin Keach

"War must be carried on systematically, and to do it you must have men of character activated by principles of honor." ~ General George Washington

"All that is required for evil to prevail is for good men to do nothing." ~ Edmund Burke

"We help believers discover and walk in their calling!" ~ John Carrette

"I only regret that I have but one life to give for my country." ~ Nathan Hale

Assumptions

I assume everyone reading this book is a born again, spirit filled believer in the Lord Jesus Christ. If that is not the case, then this short chapter is for you. There are some things that will not make sense to you if you are not born again. The Word tells us we need a savior because all have sinned. Jesus told us we had to be born again if we wanted to see the kingdom of God.

John 3:3-5 Jesus answered and said unto him, Verily, verily, I say unto thee, Except a man be born again, he cannot see the kingdom of God. 4 Nicodemus saith unto him, How can a man be born when he is old? can he enter the second time into his mother's womb, and be born? 5 Jesus answered, Verily, verily, I say unto thee, Except a man be born of water and of the Spirit, he cannot enter into the kingdom of God.

We must be born of water and the Spirit. There is no other way to walk in God's favor and power. In order to accomplish this, we must believe and obey what scripture tells us. For me, one of the easiest ways to remember the scripture verses to lead a person to salvation is the Roman Road to Salvation (also in Appendix D):

Romans 3:10 As it is written, There is none righteous, no, not one:

Romans 3:23 For all have sinned, and come short of the glory of God;

Romans 5:8 But God commendeth his love toward us, in that, while we were yet sinners, Christ died for us.

Romans 6:23 For the wages of sin is death; but the gift of God is eternal life through Jesus Christ our Lord.

Romans 10:13 For whosoever shall call upon the name of the Lord shall be saved.

Romans 10:9 That if thou shalt confess with thy mouth the Lord Jesus, and shalt believe in thine heart that God hath raised him from the dead, thou shalt be saved. 10 For with the heart man believeth unto righteousness; and with the mouth confession is made unto salvation.

You have just been presented with as clear a picture of the Gospel as I can portray. If you have not already done so, or are not sure of your salvation, then today is the day of salvation.

Deuteronomy 30:19 I call heaven and earth to record this day against you, that I have set before you life and death, blessing and cursing: therefore choose life, that both thou and thy seed may live:

2 Corinthians 6:2 (For he saith, I have heard thee in a time accepted, and in the day of salvation have I succoured thee: behold, now is the accepted time; behold, now is the day of salvation.)

If you believe Jesus Christ is the son of God, that He came and lived as a man and was crucified and put to death for your sins and mine; and that He was raised back to life three days later, then pray this prayer aloud to receive salvation and become born again:

Father God, I confess I am a sinner and I ask you to forgive me of my sins. I believe that Jesus is your son and that he came and lived and died to pay my penalty for my sins. I thank you for His work on my behalf. I believe Jesus was raised back to life and now sits at Your right hand preparing to return and gather His people. I ask You to come into my heart and help me to live as You would have me to live. In Jesus' name I pray. Amen

When we receive Jesus as our Lord, we are instantly changed in our spirits for:

2 Corinthians 5:17 Therefore if any man be in Christ, he is a new creature: old things are passed away; behold, all things are become new.

Many Christians continue to live within their physical and emotional limits and are oblivious to the new, born-again part of them that received the fullness of God. You may not feel your spirit is pure and clean before God, but it is! Believe what the Word of God tells you because God's Word is Spirit and life.

John 6:63 It is the spirit that quickeneth; the flesh profiteth nothing: the words that I speak unto you, they are spirit, and they are life.

Your spiritual stand before God is complete. Nothing can be added to it. In your spirit, you are right now as you will be throughout all eternity. Praise the Lord Jesus!

1 John 4:17 Herein is our love made perfect, that we may have boldness in the day of judgment: because as he is, so are we in this world.

The second critical component for a warrior of Christ is the baptism of the Holy Spirit. I go into this teaching later, but let me say that if you have not received the baptism of the Holy Spirit, there is nothing preventing you from doing so. You do not have to be qualified or jump through any hurdles or hoops to receive this baptism. It is for the church at large. That means everyone who is born again can receive it. The only key to receiving this baptism is to believe that it is real, that it is for you and that you can have it. If you are ready to receive the baptism of the Holy Spirit, pray aloud:

Lord Jesus, you are my Lord and Savior. I know you are the baptizer of the Holy Spirit and I ask you now to fill me with your Holy Spirit. I ask you to baptize me now with your Holy Spirit so that I can be used as your Spirit leads me. Please free me from anything that binds or hinders me – from any fear, unbelief, prejudice, or shyness so I can be free to praise you in a new language given to me by the Holy Spirit. I ask you to fill me with rivers of living water to bring life to the desert around me. In your precious and matchless name Jesus, I thank you for giving me a new language. I believe I receive it now. Amen.

Now, lift your hands and praise Jesus! Praise Him and worship

Him and yield your mouth to the Holy Spirit and believe that you will receive a new language and you will! Do not speak in your native language. Yield yourself to the presence of the Holy Spirit and begin to speak out those words that you do not understand. It may sound funny or like gibberish to you in the beginning, but just press on and continue to speak whatever the Holy Spirit gives you. In order to establish this firmly in your life, pray this way for at least fifteen minutes.

If for some reason you do not receive do not be upset. The enemy hates this and fights it. satan will tell you this is nonsense and that you are making it up, or any other lie to get you to abandon the effort. Find a spirit-filled person who will pray with you and try again.

If you did receive, then raise your hands and praise God for His loving kindness and provision. You just entered a door into the supernatural ways of God that will amaze and thrill you for eternity! Find time every day to pray in tongues, preferably an hour a day. This will build up your spirit-man and edify you! Praying in tongues is the single most important key to attaining and walking in mountain-moving faith and power!

1 Corinthians 14:4 He that speaketh in an unknown tongue edifieth himself; but he that prophesieth edifieth the church.

The last component necessary before we continue with this series is that the work of restoration must begin in you. This happens when you decide to forgive everyone who has ever hurt you in any way. You do not have to forget what was done, and you do not have to like what was done to you. And, you do not have to allow it to continue either. If you are in danger in any way either physically, mentally or spiritually – remove yourself from that situation. God does not want you to allow any abuse to continue.

Remember that forgiveness is for the one who does the forgiving.

Assumptions

While it may seem otherwise, it is not for the perpetrator or person who hurt you. When we forgive, we allow God to have full reign. We turn that person over to God and allow Him to make all things right. Our job is to simply forgive, unconditionally. Once we do that – we begin our own healing. This is a choice and a matter of our will. We choose to forgive specifically forgiving each event or incident by name and situation. Something like this:

Father, I come before you in the name of Jesus and I choose now to forgive my Uncle Joe for calling me stupid simply because I did not understand what he wanted. Forgive him Father for he did not know what he was doing or how much pain he caused me. In Jesus' name I pray. Amen.

Please note that when we withhold forgiveness toward anyone, it does not hurt that person. It only hurts us. Most of the time, the person whom we have not forgiven is completely unaware of our predicament. If they are not saved, they might be happy to know our pain is continuing. That is one reason why God tells us to forgive. Forgiveness that is withheld lingers in our soul and grows into a deep bitter pool that will become harder and harder to let go.

Once we forgive everyone who has ever hurt us, it cleanses us so we can proceed to reconciliation and restoration. Total unconditional forgiveness is a key to wholeness and wellness, and is vital to good spiritual health. Jesus modeled the prayer of forgiveness for us from the cross:

Luke 23:34 Then said Jesus, Father, forgive them; for they know not what they do…

This is known as the mercy prayer, and we can use it too to help us forgive any who have hurt us. When we forgive we are being like Jesus, and like God who is so merciful.

Matthew 5:45 That ye may be the children of your Father which is in heaven: for he maketh his sun to rise on the evil and on the good, and sendeth rain on the just and on the unjust.

When we forgive, we take all the pain and suffering the enemy meant for us to carry and we lay it down at the foot of the cross of Jesus. He is strong enough to carry it so we will not have to and He is the perfect judge who will make all things right.

Father, teach us your ways and help us be more like Jesus! Help us not carry the weight of unforgiveness in Jesus' name. Help us Father to be quick to forgive and not allow any bitter pool to develop within us. Amen.

A Call to Arms

"Cowards never won heaven. Do not claim that you are begotten of God and have His royal blood running in your veins unless you can prove your lineage by this heroic spirit: to dare to be holy in spite of men and devils." ~ William Gurnall.

"I will die for my God. I will die for my faith. It is the least I can do for Christ dying for me." ~ Cassie Bernall, Columbine High Martyr [1]

Luke 4:18 The Spirit of the Lord *is* upon me, because he hath anointed me to preach the gospel to the poor; he hath sent me to heal the brokenhearted, to preach deliverance to the captives, and recovering of sight to the blind, to set at liberty them that are bruised, 19 To preach the acceptable year of the Lord.

"Those who will not be ruled by GOD will be ruled by TYRANTS." ~ William Penn

In the Spirit, there is a battle that continually rages over each one of us. Forces of good and evil collide with great fury and contend for the souls of men. This is the battle of the ages! We are not called to be bystanders in this raging battle, but we are called to pick up our swords and join in! We are called to come up higher and join the fray! We are called to join forces and participate in our own sanctification and for the redemption and salvation of all we hold dear.

In reality, many of us are losing the battle against sin, sickness and disease, and death. We are losing the battle for our families, for our towns, cities and nations. The old enemy, satan, is busy and he knows his time is short so he has pulled out all the weapons at his disposal and he is furiously at work killing, stealing and destroying.

We live in increasingly dark days. Crisis follows after crisis. Disaster follows disaster. Fear drives the nations in their decisions. The truths that have been the spiritual foundation of western nations for centuries are now overthrown in favor of a secular society which denies the very existence of God and has no respect for His Word or His truth.

The signs all around us are clear - judgment is at hand and it is increasing in frequency, intensity and severity in a way we never dreamed of. Disasters of all types are on the rise as is the rate of acceleration in their severity and intensity. By all accounts, the world is in for a very wild ride.

March 11, 2011.[2] More than 22,000 people killed or missing when a 9.0 magnitude earthquake and resulting tsumanis struck Tohoku, Japan. The earthquake moved Honshu 2.4 m (8 ft) east and shifted the Earth on its axis by estimates of between 10 cm (4 in) and 25 cm (10 in).

January 8, 2011.[3] A mass shooting occurred near Tucson, Arizona.

A Call to Arms

Nineteen people were shot; six of those died. The event took place during a public meeting that U.S. Representative Gabrielle Giffords was holding for constituents in the Casas Adobes Safeway supermarket parking lot. She was the primary target of the shooter, was shot and received a horrific head wound but survives.

January 12, 2010.[4] An estimated 300,000 people were killed when a 7.0-magnitude earthquake struck Haiti. The devastation there has been unimaginable.

April 16, 2007.[5] The Virginia Tech massacre was a school shooting on the campus of Virginia Polytechnic Institute and State University in Blacksburg, Virginia. In two separate attacks, approximately two hours apart, the perpetrator killed 32 people and wounded 25 others before committing suicide. The massacre is the deadliest shooting incident by a single gunman in U.S. history.

December 26, 2004.[6] A magnitude 9.0 quake struck off the coast of Sumatra, triggering tsunamis that swept through the coastal regions of a dozen countries bordering the Indian Ocean. The death toll has been estimated at between 225,000 and 275,000.

April 20, 1999.[7] The Columbine High School massacre occurred in Columbine, an unincorporated area of Jefferson County, Colorado, United States, near Denver and Littleton. Two senior students, embarked on a massacre, killing 12 students and 1 teacher. They also injured 21 other students directly, and three people were injured while attempting to escape. The pair then committed suicide.

These are only a few of the incidents from recent times. And, yet, the church sleeps on. We are not armed and dangerous, nor are very many of us even aware of the activity of our enemy and his forces. Mostly, we watch these events as if we are detached from them. We sit as prey waiting to be harvested by unseen hands and forces who hate us with an intensity that would shock you.

If we cannot humble ourselves after witnessing terrible natural and manmade disasters, what will it take to open our eyes to what is really happening? Think of these facts:

- God's expulsion from society in the name of political correctness
- The whole world turning to secularism and materialism
- The church growing worldlier than the world itself
- The meteoric rise of violence and apathy
- The rise and acceptance of magic and of witchcraft
- The rise and veneration of lust in all its forms
- Morality has become a liability
- The Bible is no longer accepted as God's Word
- The church is in a free fall decline of epic proportions
- A day when everything that can be shaken is being shaken
- Humility, honestly and integrity are viewed as weakness
- When society continues its business without a single God pause, without a thought that God will not be mocked
- People are referred to as units once again (much like the Nazi's did prior to WWII)
- Evil is called good, and good is called evil

It seems certain now we have crossed a line into a spiritual stupor that no amount of divine mercy can awaken us from. Even the church does not want to hear the truth anymore. They would much rather have their ears tickled. Deception, lies and subterfuge are so prevalent very few can discern the real truth when they hear it.

It is inconceivable that even 20 years ago, we would ever see the devastation, general mayhem and carnage we see on the news today on a nearly daily basis. We have become numb to it. Further, everywhere we look, people are calling good evil, and evil good. There is no right anymore, only naked raw lust and desire for power, money and wealth, and personal pleasure. All of this is happening at the expense of those less fortunate without regard for human decency or morality. It is revolting and shocking.

Sometimes I feel like a time traveler who has arrived back in the 21st century from a long trip to another time; a time where people really cared about one another, and where duty, honor and respect for each other really meant something; and, a time when material things were just that. They were tools or objects to use and nothing more. No one craved them or would hurt another person to get them. A time when we did not lock our doors mostly because we did not have any locks on them and our neighbors looked out for us.

2 Peter 2:7-8 And delivered just Lot, vexed with the filthy conversation of the wicked: 8 (For that righteous man dwelling among them, in seeing and hearing, vexed his righteous soul from day to day with their unlawful deeds;)

Then, sometimes I feel like Lot whom scripture says sat at the gate of Sodom sorely vexed by all that was going on around him. I used to wonder why Lot did not just pack up and leave Sodom long before the angels came to fetch him and his family. Now I think I understand why. After all, where would he go? If we decided to leave our homes, to where would we flee to escape the evils of this world?

I often wonder, what happened to America? Where have all the good people gone? Why is everyone so greedy, so jealous of one another, so hell bent on attaining more stuff, so obsessed with how they and their families *look*? Now, we have several locks on every door, locks on the windows and sometimes bars on both. Home invasions are not only on the increase in a dramatic way, but now they are old news and are not nearly as newsworthy as they were even a few years ago.

There is more shocking information from the United States where approximately six million pregnancies occur each year but only two out of three of these babies survive and are born due to abortion, miscarriages, stillbirth and other complications. Of those born, which is about four million, nearly two million, or one of every two will be born exposed to either alcohol or illegal drugs while in the womb.⁸

When a drug exposed baby is born, the state takes them from the hospital and removes them from their parents' custody. This is happening at an alarming rate. Many of these little ones are never reunited with their birth parents because their parents are incapable of overcoming the addictions in their own lives. So, they end up in foster care, if they are lucky. Many do not, and will be relegated to orphanages and other state run boarding homes that are run by people paid far too little to attract the best. Most of these people mean well, but are so overworked and underpaid it is literally a crying shame. This is creating an entire generation of people that has no one to love them or teach them right from wrong. A godless secular society that does not believe in right or wrong is now trying to raise these children. What do you think they will be like when they are young adults?

Maybe instead of hiding from what is happening or running away, we should take a stand right where we are? Maybe we should drive a stake in the ground and attach our leg to it and declare here I stand or fall, but it is up to you Lord and I trust you to see me through?

We are standing on the edge of eternity, and we are the generation that will see the culmination of all things! God is not surprised by what is happening in the world today. He does not wake up wringing His hands in worry about what is going to happen next. He told us from the beginning what the end was going to be like, and its here! Yet, where great darkness abounds, light abounds even more.

Romans 5:20 Moreover the law entered, that the offence might abound. But where sin abounded, grace did much more abound:

We who are His will have the awesome privilege of seeing God's plan come to completion in all its fullness. The great men of God from the past longed to see what we will see and to hear what we will hear, but did not.

Matthew 13:17 For verily I say unto you, That many prophets and righteous *men* have desired to see *those things* which ye see, and have not seen *them*; and to hear *those things* which ye hear, and have not heard *them*.

We will see the return of Jesus in all His glory and majesty, and I know many of us can hardly wait for that to happen. Yet, He told us to press on, reaching out to the lost, the hurt, the sick, the maimed and the dead until He returned.

Matthew 10:7 And as ye go, preach, saying, The kingdom of heaven is at hand. 8 Heal the sick, cleanse the lepers, raise the dead, cast out devils: freely ye have received, freely give.

We are part of a Golden Chain[9] of men that once enlightened by the Gospel, now reaches out to help our families and our neighbors to take off the blinders that blind them so they can open their eyes to really see their true purpose and calling (See Appendix A for Demos Shakarian's vision). This is both a terrible and an awesome calling. Terrible in that if we fail to answer this call, we will be held accountable for the blood of those we failed to warn. Yet, this call is also incredibly awesome in that we will be greatly and richly rewarded by seeing the rescue of so many from the clutches of the enemy and his forces as the last great revival and harvest is about ready to begin.

Proverbs 11:30 The fruit of the righteous *is* a tree of life; and he that winneth souls *is* wise.

James 5:20 Let him know, that he which converteth the sinner from the error of his way shall save a soul from death, and shall hide a multitude of sins.

Jude 1:23 And others save with fear, pulling *them* out of the fire; hating even the garment spotted by the flesh.

In the world today, there is a group of men and women whose sole aim is to reach out to the lost, the hurting, the imprisoned and the bound. Their aim is to set them free, to hold Jesus high and glorify God in accordance with the same scripture Jesus quoted when he returned from forty days in the desert:

Luke 4:18 The Spirit of the Lord *is* upon me, because he hath anointed me to preach the gospel to the poor; he hath sent me to heal the brokenhearted, to preach deliverance to the captives, and recovering of sight to the blind, to set at liberty them that are bruised, 19 To preach the acceptable year of the Lord.

These people belong to two groups called The Full Gospel Business Men's Fellowship International (FGBMFI) and Woman's Aglow, and they take this commission very, very seriously. The men of the Full Gospel Business Men's Fellowship, International come from nearly every denomination and they hold several things in common:

We Believe (simply stated):

That God exists.
That He is the Creator of the Universe.
That God is the Father of mankind.
He created the first man and woman in His image.
That God's plan for mankind is GOOD!

That Jesus Christ is the Son of God.
He was born into this world to redeem mankind back to a proper relationship with the Father.
Through His death and resurrection, we can receive salvation and are reconciled to God.

That the precious Holy Spirit of God is working in our lives today to bring about the will of the Father.
And I am personally seeking His fullness in my life.

That the Holy Bible is the Word of God to mankind.

This is the common ground between the members of FGBMFI. We believe all who believe these tenets are our brothers, and we love, honor and cherish them as such.

These men and women, and others like them are like the knights of old, Knights of the Round Table – if you will permit the analogy. We come together to gather strength, get respite from the darkness we so often face and to sharpen our skills and spiritual eyesight. We gather to honor our King, Jesus, and to praise Him for His goodness and His kindness to us and those to whom we minister. We gather to plan, to decree God's will for the future, to heal and to train replacements for those who have fallen along the way. We gather strength from one another and from our common bond of brotherly love one for another. We humble ourselves before our Lord and each other and prepare to re-enter the fray.

Come! Join us! God is still looking for a few good men who will submit to His Lordship and care for His sheep... Again, I say Come! Arise , become Men.

>   Arise, Mighty Warriors!

>   Arise, Men of Honor!

>   Arise, Men of Integrity!

>   Arise, Men of Valor!

The greatest battle of all time awaits you!

In the Declaration of Independence our forefathers pledged their lives, their fortunes and their sacred honor in support of the United

States of America. Can we do any less now for our countries, our communities and our families?

Father, I pray for great courage and great determination for everyone who answers your call. Teach us through your Spirit to be men of honor, men of integrity and men of valor. In Jesus' name I pray. Amen.

Why Now?

"Give me a hundred men who fear nothing but sin, and desire nothing but God, and I will shake the world. I care not a straw whether they be clergymen or laymen; and, such alone will overthrow the kingdom of satan and build up the kingdom of God on earth." ~ John Wesley

Ezekiel 22:30 And I sought for a man among them, that should make up the hedge, and stand in the gap before me for the land, that I should not destroy it: but I found none.

Micah 3:8 But truly I am full of power by the spirit of the LORD, and of judgment, and of might, to declare unto Jacob his transgression, and to Israel his sin. Here is a little background on me and how I came to write this book:

I have believed in God and that Jesus was His son as long as I can remember, but I did not have a personal relationship with Jesus until about the mid 1990's. I was happy doing my own thing, living my life, etc. I felt God around me most of the time and was aware of His presence even if I could not explain it to anyone. I had no idea how miserable I really was. I was radically born again while reading a paperback version of *The Way, the Living Bible*. My mother Cassie Keyte made me promise I would read it and I honor her now in that it was the catalyst that saved both me and all I hold dear!

I did not know it at the time, but all the women in my life were praying for me every day! My wife, my sister, my mother, aunts and cousins were all holding me up before God and asking Him to change my heart. It worked! It took some time, but it really worked. God is always faithful. As I said, I was reading *The Way* and asking God daily to reveal Himself to me through His word. He did! As I read, I would have questions like "What is the secret place of the Most High?," "What about such and such..." and so on. A day or two later, the verse or verses I needed to answer those questions would illuminate on the page I was reading and lift up off the page. That really got my attention! I realized God was talking to me, and answering my prayers!

What an amazing adventure and answer to my prayer! God is so good! I carried that bible around with me everywhere I went for three years. Almost wore it completely out. But, I had an opportunity to share that story with a young man and then I made a gift of that bible to him so it could do the same for him. What an honor that was.

I watched Charles Stanley on television for my spiritual nourishment rather than attending any church. I really was not sure what kind of Christian I was. Mom was a Baptist and dad's people were all Lutherans and I would attend many churches from both denominations, and other denominations as well but the God I discovered while reading *The Way* was more personal and much closer than I had heard about in any of these churches.

I spent several years reading the bible every day and watching Dr. Stanley and Word of Faith pastors, just growing in the Lord and in my knowledge of Him. One day I ran into a lady who told me she was a prophet of God and that she was sent to me to teach me about deliverance ministry. This changed everything. I started getting really serious about my relationship with God and questioning Christian history, the various denominations and how we ended up where we are today. Some of the answers were surprising, even alarming. This study continued for about nine months and culminated with my baptism in the Holy Spirit.

As I went about living my life and doing everyday mundane things, the Spirit would whisper to me "that one's dead," and He did that sometimes for weeks at a time. I would hear "that one's dead," or "that one is lost with no hope" of redemption or salvation. This always left me in a near state of panic. I felt I must do more, in fact much more to reach out to the lost, and to those on the broad road to hell.

Or, I would see the shelves in stores empty (in my mind's eye – my spiritual eye). I often thought this spoke of a future famine and it very well may, but what I am sensing now is that the shelves are empty because they do not contain anything of value. We place too much emphasis on the here and now, living and the necessity of things that do not amount to much when they are compared to eternity.

What I finally realized was the Lord was separating me from the world for His purposes. Most people do not understand how we can set Jesus as our first priority, but it usually does not happen overnight. The Spirit of God woos us and draws us closer and closer, a little here and a little there until before we know it, Jesus is everything to us. It really is quite amazing. It is often very unpleasant while we are going through this process, but looking back on it now, I have nothing but admiration, affection and awe for the Holy Spirit and His work in, on and through me.

I have been studying and seeking the Lord hard now for over fifteen years. And, he has met me and blessed me beyond my wildest expectations. He has delivered me from addictions, pride, arrogance and the wickedness of a selfish existence. I am His – wholly and outright. I still stumble on occasion but for the most part – I live above the snake line – not because of my own righteousness but because of Him – He who is in me! Christ in me – the hope of glory! Praise God!

Colossians 1:27 To whom God would make known what is the riches of the glory of this mystery among the Gentiles; which is Christ in you, the hope of glory:

This work, this book, began years ago before I was saved. I can see God's hand in my life with total clarity now that I am looking back at the life I have led through spirit-filled eyes, and with an awareness of God's ways. What an amazing journey it has been! God is so good every single day! I know I say that a lot, but He really is you know.

I joined a group of men, called the Full Gospel Business Men's Fellowship International (FGBMFI) after reading a book named *"They SPEAK with OTHER TONGUES,"* written by John Sherrill, and receiving the Baptism of the Holy Spirit. In the book, John Sherrill mentioned the FGBMFI group several times and I asked the Lord one day "If these fellows still exist, I would like to meet them. I think I am supposed to join them."

Mind you, I am not a joiner. If I cannot put everything I have into it, I will just stay out of it. I am also not a very good spectator either. I loved sports as a youth and played everything I could, but I cannot stand to sit and watch a game on television. If I cannot be in there amongst them so to speak, I want no part of it. That is just my nature.

Anyway, in a week or two, I saw an ad in a weekly trade paper or some other advertisement for the Full Gospel Business Men's Fellowship International's local meeting. This occurred on a regular weekly basis. I was ecstatic and called the number listed. I introduced myself and found out where they met. I started attending local weekly meetings and have been very active in our chapter for the last seven years. I know God led me to the FGBMFI – supernaturally. And, again He answered my prayer. Praise God for His mercy and loving kindness!

I am now a Lifetime member of the FGBMFI, and President of our local chapter. I found the most wonderful men I have ever known in this organization: men who love God, who really love Jesus and who are willing to humble themselves before Him, to reach out to the lost and dying, and who regularly lay their lives down to help and minister to others. These are men who can tell each other they love one another and no one feels weird.

These men taught me how to evangelize, how to pray for healing and deliverance, how to pray fervently and purposefully, and how to walk this Christian life in power rather than timidity. We work in the local county jail and local prisons ministering to people who are bound by the enemy of our souls; we do hospital visitations and we witness for Jesus everywhere we go. We see God at work in people's lives daily and great miracles every week. We man a booth at local county fairs named "The God Mobile," where we evangelize fair goers. This in itself is an amazing story, but I will save that for another day.

At the 2011 Arizona Men's Advance for the Full Gospel Business Men's Fellowship International, I was asked to speak a word of prophesy and this is what came out of my mouth as I yielded to the Holy Spirit:

"Arise, Ish Elohim! Arise, Mighty Men of God! It is time to shake off the chains and shackles that held you for so long. It is time to rise up and take the land back from the enemy and his forces of evil. It is time to reach out to the lost, the hurt, the sick and the bound and help them become over comers and active members of the kingdom of our God. This the last great battle for men's souls! It is upon us and we must rise up and wage war now!"

There was more, but that was the gist of it. Since the advance, the Lord has been downloading the information in this book to me on a daily basis; always with power, and with distinct clarity and purpose. I am sure this is His doing as I did not have all this laid out and organized in my mind. I had no notion of writing a book and yet, here I am. And, I am sure this is my current assignment – to get this message out to people everywhere.

I asked the Lord what he wanted to call this effort, and after a few days, the answer that came to me was *"The Warrior Anointing."* I had never heard of such a thing. I was familiar with anointing, but not with a warrior anointing. I researched this and found many books that touch on the subject, but none that seemed to fully grasp what the Lord was conveying to my spirit. I have listed several of these in the Recommended Reading section at the end of this book. I found dreams and prophesies that touched on it, but they still did not express what I feel the Lord wants to say at this time.

This is bigger than a onetime event. This represents a change to the way the church lives its life on a daily basis. The kingdom of God is not sometime in the future. From the beginning, I was taught the kingdom of God was now and not yet. I submit the time is now. Eternity for believers does not start at physical death. It began when we were saved! We are His kingdom and we are on the road through to eternity right now! It is a work in progress in our hearts – in our spirits. I am not claiming that this book is a "Thus sayeth the Lord" kind of thing, but it is His ideas, His agenda and His work through me. I will convey as best I can what I feel the Lord is trying to say to His people at this point in time. Bless His Holy Name!

It is time to reclaim that which the enemy has stolen. He came to kill, steal and destroy and it is time we took the battle to him. Jesus came that we might have life, and life more abundantly (John 10:10). It is time to cut the chains loose and become the mighty men of valor we are called to be: men of honor, of integrity, of courage and of wisdom. It is time to break off the chains and walk in the authority Jesus has bestowed upon us. It is time to become the Mighty Men of Yeshua!

We need to move away from denominationalism. We need to go back to basics. If a man believes that Jesus is the Christ and the son of God. If he believes that Jesus came and lived as a man, and was without sin. If he believes Jesus went to the cross to bear his penalty for his sins as well as for yours and mine. If he believes Jesus was crucified and died, was buried and raised back to life through His power and the power of the Holy Spirit. If he believes that Jesus is now at the right hand of the Father in heaven and that He is returning soon for His church; then we are brothers and I will love him as my brother.

I am pretty sure none of us has it all right or knows all there is to know about God, about Jesus or about the Holy Spirit. As I have said many times, my theology is continuing to evolve as my depth of understanding about God, His Word and His ways continues to deepen. I am not the same man I was ten years ago, and my ideas and notions about God have grown tremendously in that time. We should be able to agree to disagree on some things and not nitpick over minutia. If we agree on the basic principles of Jesus' divinity, His mission and His return, we are pretty close. I know some will see this as heresy, but that is just how I feel.

Courage is the secret weapon to a fulfilling and blessed life. For, without courage, you cannot fully develop and grow in mind, body and spirit. This one key ingredient defines who we really are. We must never change for the mainstream. If you are talented, resilient and stay strong, the mainstream will come to you. Do the thing you fear and the death of that fear is certain.

Philippians 4:13 I can do all things through Christ who strengthens me.

I was led, by God, to this place through the wonderful men and ministry of the Full Gospel Business Men's Fellowship International, but I am not naive enough to believe this is limited by any means to any particular group or subgroup of men or women. By the way, I refer to men mostly in this work but that applies equally to men and women. We are all called to a higher place and a higher calling in Christ Jesus!

The only limitation on this call to arms is the openness of the hearts and minds of those who will receive it. God will use everyone who will respond to His call. Jesus said whosoever will...

Mark 8:34 And when he had called the people *unto him* with his disciples also, he said unto them, Whosoever will come after me, let him deny himself, and take up his cross, and follow me.

As I said earlier, this is all God's doing – His thoughts and ideas, His work. So, to the Lord be all the glory, honor and praise forever more! I am one of His vessels trying to convey His message. I have seen very recent prophesies from Cindy Jacobs, Rick Joyner and Bobby Conner and others that confirm this work.

Dear heavenly Father, I pray that this message resonates with every heart that reads it. I pray dear Holy Spirit, please touch everyone reading this and give them a sense of urgency and immediacy about the days and times we live in. Help us to rise up and answer this call and honor you. I pray for a quickening of our Spirits and a certainty that this is the road we should take. And, I pray for great courage, great wisdom, great joy and great peace as we venture forth in your name Jesus! Amen.

The Call of God

"Some want to live within the sound of church or chapel bell; I want to run a rescue shop within a yard of hell." ~ C. T. Studd

Deuteronomy 7:6 For you are a holy people unto the LORD your God: the LORD your God has chosen you to be a special people unto himself, above all people that are upon the face of the earth.

1 Corinthians 16:13 Watch ye, stand fast in the faith, quit you like men, be strong.

2 Timothy 2:4 No man that wars entangles himself with the affairs of this life; that he may please him who has chosen him to be a soldier.

Throughout the Bible, there are accounts of mighty men of valor, of warriors, men and women of honor. These accounts always intrigued me and I have spent many an hour contemplating their significance. God never called His people to be timid, or lukewarm. In every case, God asked His people to come up higher, to live holy and righteous lives before their brethren.

As a young boy, I often had dreams where I was part of a large company of people who were trekking through some wilderness in search of sanctuary. I did not understand very much about God, but I often felt His presence with me. I knew in my spirit that I was supposed to do great things. Yet, I had no idea what that might be. As I grew older, the things of the world drew me away and hardened me in so many ways. I lost the innocence of my youth and my sense of wonder. I learned to conform to society and what others expected of me.

I believe this is what happens to so many people. I recently had a counseling session with a young man who told me he always had the idea he was supposed to do great things for God. He said that he could feel the power coursing in him and struggling to burst forth from his abdomen. He had dreams where he was told he was supposed to be a soldier for Jesus Christ. Yet, he had no idea of how to tap into that or to see it come to pass in his life. People thought he was weird.

I have heard this same story from so many people that I am convinced this is no coincidence. Rather, I believe this is God's original purpose for many of us! But, our enemy and the world have stolen this destiny from us. Our original purpose and destiny is to reign in this life as kings and priests, but we have been disillusioned, depressed and deprived of the wonder of it all. Instead of having steak for breakfast, we have been given mush.

If you have ever had a dream or vision where you were told you were to lead people, or serve people, or teach people or in any way minister to people; you have probably had a call from God on your life. You see, we are created by God with a specific destiny in mind. God has a plan for each one of us. We are created in His image, and we will live forever in one place or another. That is why we often feel as though we are like a fish out of water. If we are not being about or living that destiny in our lives, we cannot be fulfilled.

God does not call us in our strength, but often calls us in a way we never thought He would. Usually, we have not given it very much thought at all. But God loves to display His strength through our weakness so often times if the call on our life does not really stretch us, it may not be from God. Moreover, in many cases, the target of God's call to arms was reluctant – often very reluctant to see themselves as men of valor. Moses was very reluctant:

Exodus 3:10 Come now therefore, and I will send thee unto Pharaoh, that thou mayest bring forth my people the children of Israel out of Egypt. 11 And Moses said unto God, Who *am* I, that I should go unto Pharaoh, and that I should bring forth the children of Israel out of Egypt?

God told Joshua that every place he set his foot was to be his, and then in three separate instances to be strong and of a good courage:

Joshua 1:3 Every place that the sole of your foot shall tread upon, that have I given unto you, as I said unto Moses.

Joshua 1:6 <u>Be strong and of a good courage</u>: for unto this people shalt thou divide for an inheritance the land, which I sware unto their fathers to give them. 7 Only <u>be thou strong and very courageous</u>, that thou mayest observe to do according to all the law, which Moses my servant commanded thee: turn not from it *to* the right hand or *to* the left, that thou mayest prosper whithersoever thou goest.

Joshua 1:9 Have not I commanded thee? <u>Be strong and of a good courage</u>; be not afraid, neither be thou dismayed: for the LORD thy God *is* with thee whithersoever thou goest.

I strongly feel those words, "be strong and of a good courage" are meant for us today too. Gideon was threshing wheat at midnight so the Midianites would not see him and was convinced he was the least in his father's house:

Judges 6:12 And the angel of the LORD appeared unto him, and said unto him, The LORD *is* with thee, thou mighty man of valour. 13 And Gideon said unto him, Oh my Lord, if the LORD be with us, why then is all this befallen us? and where *be* all his miracles which our fathers told us of, saying, Did not the LORD bring us up from Egypt? but now the LORD hath forsaken us, and delivered us into the hands of the Midianites. 14 And the LORD looked upon him, and said, Go in this thy might, and thou shalt save Israel from the hand of the Midianites: have not I sent thee? 15 And he said unto him, Oh my Lord, wherewith shall I save Israel? behold, my family *is* poor in Manasseh, and I *am* the least in my father's house.

Conversely, there is the family of the Rechabites. God told Jeremiah to call them to the house of the Lord to speak to them and give them wine to drink. They came but refused to drink the wine.

Jeremiah 35:6 But they said, We will drink no wine: for Jonadab the son of Rechab our father commanded us, saying, Ye shall drink no wine, *neither* ye, nor your sons for ever: 7 Neither shall ye build house, nor sow seed, nor plant vineyard, nor have *any*: but all your days ye shall dwell in tents; that ye may live many days in the land where ye *be* strangers. 8 Thus have we obeyed the voice of Jonadab the son of Rechab our father in all that he hath charged us, to drink no wine all our days, we, our wives, our sons, nor our daughters; 9 Nor to build houses for us to dwell in: neither have we vineyard, nor field, nor seed: 10 But we have dwelt in tents, and have obeyed, and done according to all that Jonadab our father commanded us.

What integrity! What courage and faithfulness! God was so pleased with them and their faithfulness He sent Jeremiah back to them to tell them they would always have a man to stand before God forever:

Jeremiah 35:19 Therefore thus saith the LORD of hosts, the God of Israel; Jonadab the son of Rechab shall not want a man to stand before me for ever.

In the natural, none of these men had anything that qualified them as mighty men of God. Yet, God saw something in each one that He could use and later did use to affect a great many people. God is not dependent on our skill or ability. In fact, He often calls people who are uniquely unqualified for the task He calls them to.

Who was the mightiest warrior recorded in the Old Testament? Why King David, of course. Though there were many mighty men recorded in the Bible, only one stands out as a warrior of warriors.

1 Samuel 21:11 - Saul hath slain his thousands, and David his ten thousands?

David's reaction to Goliath was that he trusted in the power God and of the Holy Spirit. The devil does not respect our abilities, only the anointing of the Spirit. The anointed warrior does not fight in his own strength. Instead he fights in the strength of God; he learns submission to the influence of the Holy Spirit and then becomes a powerful instrument in God's hands. Those who fight in the flesh make lots of noise and put on a great show, but bear no fruit. Jesus said it clearly:

John 3:6 That which is born of the flesh is flesh; and that which is born of the Spirit is spirit.

Only what is born of the Spirit works in God's kingdom. The apostle Paul taught us that the weapons of God are not carnal but mighty through God:

2 Corinthians 10:3 For though we walk in the flesh, we do not war after the flesh: 4 (For the weapons of our warfare *are* not carnal, but mighty through God to the pulling down of strongholds;)

These weapons are powerful and effective to destroy spiritual strongholds. If our weapons are not mighty through God, our efforts, tenacity, and good intentions will be useless to deliver anyone from captivity. Also, the outward appearance of a warrior is not what counts either; when David killed Goliath, he did not look anything like a soldier. What truly counts is the Spirit that works and moves in, through and with us.

Psalms 44:3 For they got not the land in possession by their own sword, neither did their own arm save them: but thy right hand, and thine arm, and the light of thy countenance, because thou hadst a favour unto them.

It is not because of our sword or our might that we conquer the land, free the captives and bind up the brokenhearted. It is because of the power of God's presence through His anointing on His chosen ones.

David's mighty men are mentioned in several places in scripture. Mostly, they were mercenaries and outcasts, people who had been marginalized and set aside as good for nothing. Under David's leadership, they became the greatest fighting force the world had ever known. They loved their king and would do great exploits for him! Here are a few details of their exploits from 2 Samuel 23:8-23:

Adino the Eznite: he slew eight hundred, with his spear at one time

Shammah: defended a field of lentils against Philistines

Abishai: he slew three hundred, with his spear at one time

Benaiah: he slew two lion like men of Moab and a lion in a pit

Imagine yourself as one of David's mighty men – renowned for your ability, tenacity and fearlessness. Is not this one of our dreams from youth? Every man was once a boy who dreamed of saving the damsel in distress, fighting evil and saving the world; all in a days' work so to speak. Along the way, we have become tired, disenchanted and downright skeptical of our abilities and our capacity to do anything honorable, much less heroic.

But, it does not have to be that way! God called Moses when he was eighty years old to go back to Egypt and free the Israelite people. Nehemiah was the king's cup bearer, a slave and wine taster and God chose him to rebuild the wall around Jerusalem. Joseph was a dreamy eyed boy with very little common sense when God first touched him and started giving him dreams. Look at the Lord's disciples. Peter, Andrew, James and John were fisherman, and Matthew was a tax collector. Clearly, once the call of God touches a person, God empowers that person with His Spirit and His anointing.

This is important, God does not call the qualified, He qualifies the called! The Lord thru Haggai tells Zerubbabel to be strong for He is with him:

Haggai 2:4 Yet now be strong, O Zerubbabel, saith the LORD; and be strong, O Joshua, son of Josedech, the high priest; and be strong, all ye people of the land, saith the LORD, and work: for I am with you, saith the LORD of hosts:

Nehemiah told his people do not be afraid, remember the Lord who is great and terrible, and fight for your brothers, your wives and children and for your homes! Nehemiah told his men to work with a tool in one hand and a weapon in the other:

Nehemiah 4:14 And I looked, and rose up, and said unto the nobles, and to the rulers, and to the rest of the people, Be not ye afraid of them: remember the Lord, *which is* great and terrible, and fight for your brethren, your sons, and your daughters, your wives, and your houses.

Nehemiah 4:17 They which builded on the wall, and they that bare burdens, with those that laded, *everyone* with one of his hands wrought in the work, and with the other *hand* held a weapon.

When I was first saved, and very enthusiastic about the Lord, I surrendered all to the Lord and asked God to tell me what He wanted to do with my life. Very shortly, in a dream, I was told to read Nehemiah. So, I did that; again, and again and again. Before I was mature in the Lord, I did not get it. But, now it makes perfect sense to me. The second half of Nehemiah 4:14 seems to be my call: "Be not ye afraid of them: remember the Lord, *which is* great and terrible, and fight for your brethren, your sons, and your daughters, your wives, and your houses."

It seems God has always been looking for a few good men (sound familiar?): men who will not be afraid to face whatever is thrown at them; men who will live by integrity and honor; men who do the right thing even if it costs them their very lives.

Father, Isaiah declared in Isaiah 6:8, 'Here I am, send me.' We pray you will train us, equip us and send us. Teach us your ways Father and help us to walk in your light and in your way full of your Holy Spirit being led of your Holy Spirit every day of our lives. In the name of Jesus I pray. Amen.

Courage

"When Christ calls a man, he bids him come and die." ~ Dietrich Bonhoeffer

Revelation 12:11 And they overcame him by the blood of the Lamb, and by the word of their testimony; and they loved not their lives unto the death.

1 Corinthians 16:13 Watch ye, stand fast in the faith, quit you like men, be strong.

Have you ever read the obituaries and noticed how people are described there? Most often, people are described in death by the work they performed while they were alive. School teacher, soldier, railroad engineer and the like are typical of any obituary. You will never see - lazy servant of the Lord, lukewarm servant of God, road (retired on active duty) scholar, couch potato, etc... Oftentimes, their eulogy centers on one notable event in their lives that happened when they were in their prime. Occasionally, you might see an obituary where the person was commended as having served faithfully as a school teacher or other public servant for forty years, or something along these lines. It is hard to imagine when we are young that we will grow old and die someday.

Further, very few people ever consider their life as a whole. Before I was born again, I never looked at my life from beginning to end as if it mattered a great deal. But, it does! Before I became a servant of the Lord, I was only concerned about my next paycheck and living in a day to day kind of way that satisfied my most immediate needs and desires but bore little lasting fruit. Yet, what a person stands for matters a great deal. Actually, it is everything. Jesus put it in the proper perspective:

Mark 8:36 For what shall it profit a man, if he shall gain the whole world, and lose his own soul?

Yet, very few people will rise up and serve the Lord with abandon, with everything they have in their hand or their hearts. When the end comes - and, it is coming - what will they have to show for it? Empty phrases and empty promises for most of them I am afraid. What a shame! Rather, I would like my obituary to read - Great Warrior for the Most High! A man who loved much! One of Jesus' Mighty Men who gave everything for the Kingdom of God!

What I hope to accomplish in this book is to convey to men that they can be what they dreamed about as children. We can accomplish all things through Christ who dwells in us! We can make a very real difference in the lives of the people we encounter in our daily walk with the Lord.

Philippians 4:13 I can do all things through Christ which strengtheneth me.

It is not by our might or our power, because frankly we do not have any power at all. What we have, we have through grace. We cannot rely on our own strength, our own knowledge, or our own insightfullness or great wisdom. We must rely on the Spirit of Life, the precious Holy Spirit.

Zechariah 4:6 Then he answered and spake unto me, saying, This *is* the word of the LORD unto Zerubbabel, saying, Not by might, nor by power, but by my spirit, saith the LORD of hosts.

We can become men of valor, men of honor and men of high integrity. We can save the damsel in distress, in fact her whole family from the evils of this world. We can be light bearers of the true light – Jesus, Yeshua Ha-Mashiach the Holy Anointed One of Israel.

What stands between us and living on the warrior path? Consider Elisha, who became Elijah's apprentice:

1 Kings 19:19 So he departed thence, and found Elisha the son of Shaphat, who *was* plowing *with* twelve yoke *of oxen* before him,

and he with the twelfth: and Elijah passed by him, and cast his mantle upon him. 20 And he left the oxen, and ran after Elijah, and said, Let me, I pray thee, kiss my father and my mother, and *then* I will follow thee. And he said unto him, Go back again: for what have I done to thee? 21 And he returned back from him, and took a yoke of oxen, and slew them, and boiled their flesh with the instruments of the oxen, and gave unto the people, and they did eat. Then he arose, and went after Elijah, and ministered unto him.

Elisha was plowing with 12 yoke of oxen, twenty-four oxen! He must have been a very wealthy man. Most people of that time and area probably plowed with donkeys or at most one yoke of oxen if they were well to do. When Elijah cast his mantle over Elisha, he was saying follow me and you will be like me for I will train you. Elisha ran after him and asked that he be allowed to return and kiss his father and mother. Elijah tells him to go, and consider what he has done to him. I think he was telling Elisha to go and count the cost before deciding what to do:

Luke 14:27 And whosoever doth not bear his cross, and come after me, cannot be my disciple. 28 For which of you, intending to build a tower, sitteth not down first, and counteth the cost, whether he have *sufficient* to finish *it*?

Elisha not only calculated the cost, he destroyed what he had, his living, so he would not be looking back! He killed a yoke of oxen, used the plow to build a fire and boiled or roasted the meat of the oxen and fed his town! Then, he took off after Elijah. Jesus told us not to look back:

Luke 9:62 And Jesus said unto him, No man, having put his hand to the plough, and looking back, is fit for the kingdom of God.

So, Elisha gave up everything to follow Elijah. We should be willing to do no less for Jesus. There is a principle concerning this, and it involves putting God and Jesus first in our life. If we will be His, really His, then He must be the first priority in our lives. God desperately wants you; but He will not share you with anyone or anything. Hear His call to you today, "Come, follow Me." We are to destroy all that holds us back and take up our cross and follow Him now.

Luke 5:28 And he left all, rose up, and followed him.

When this life is done, and we look back at what we have accomplished, we will only be proud of those things that are of eternal value. This includes helping people who could not help themselves, leading people to see Jesus for who He really is, loving the unlovely and teaching others how to overcome sin and evil. I tell young folks all the time that I have more years behind me in this body than I have ahead of me. I try to ensure I am spending my time on the things that really matter; things that have eternal consequences and I am very aware of my own character and how I want that to be perceived by those that follow me.

It is often been said, "Character is what you do when nobody is watching. Character is how you treat people who can do absolutely nothing for you. Character is how you react when the pressure is on. Character is deciding beforehand that you are going to do the right thing."

Every day we are faced with decisions - many of which are made when no one is watching. So let us decide right now to do the right thing in every situation because character really does matter. Our character and our honor do matter. When we arrive in heaven, we want to hear, "well done thou good and faithful servant." After all, we represent the King of Kings and the Lord of Lords. As His men and women, His representatives, we should live above reproach.

We can overcome the addictions, temptations and evils thrown at us in this world. We can rise above the snake line and become overcomers by learning how to walk in the Spirit. We can take back our homes, our neighborhoods, our towns and cities, our states and even the nations of this world for our king – Jesus! Every place we set our foot can become Kingdom Territory for our King Yeshua!

The Warrior Anointing, destiny awaits

Dear heavenly Father, please help me this day to lay aside all of the things that hold me back so that in the power of your presence within me, the precious Holy Spirit, I can and will fully follow You. Teach me to be a man of integrity and honor. In Christ's name I pray, Amen.

Life – is about People

~ Alan B. Keyte

"I have decided to follow Jesus, Tho' no one joins me, still I will follow, The world behind me, the cross before me, No turning back, no turning back." ~ S. Sundar Singh

Life really is about people. For each of us, it is about becoming who God created us to be. For the world in general, it is about caring for our brothers. Those who walk through life only concerned about what they can get are missing so much more that life has to offer.

We often miss the details of some of Gods best, simply because we are too busy making a living, or studying or something when the greatest moments of our lives simply slip away from us. I have always enjoyed watching people as they go about their lives making a living, playing, loving and striving to overcome the obstacles placed in their way. People are so amazing and very funny too.

Have you ever seen a matched pair of horses work as a team? Or, have you ever watched a pair of perfectly matched sled dogs pulling a sled? There is a simplicity about their combined efforts that is beautiful to behold and marvelous to contemplate. There is another connotation that implies matched only in size and color. I am not referring to that. What I am talking about is more related to working together. A good swing dog will swing the whole team around behind him in a turn, but you have to have a calm, strong wheel dog to keep the sled from tipping over when you do turn. They work together to get the job done. Matched pairs of draft animals have long been sought after for their ability to get the job done and compensate for each other's weaknesses.

When two people really know one another well and work together for a common cause, it is a wondrous thing to see. How they complement one another so perfectly; one knows or anticipates what the other will need and is there with what will be needed just in time to handle their part of the chore. It is like watching a master mason building a wall and his helper keeping the bricks and mud at hand so he never has to lose a step or miss a beat – perfect harmony; simple, yet elegant.

That is the way our relationship should be with the Holy Spirit. He knows us perfectly, even better than we know ourselves and He is always there when we need Him. Just the other day, I was approaching a car that was facing out of a driveway and the Holy Spirit immediately warned me to be careful. I slowed down a little as I approached the car and then when I was within thirty feet of it, it suddenly swung out in front of me from the right. I reacted instantly and yanked the car hard to the left while applying the brake. I did not even have time to hit the horn. Somehow, we got past him without being hit but it was very, very close. There is no way I could have reacted so quickly if I had not been warned, or if I was not sensitive to that *still small voice* that speaks within me.

Life is about people. It is very simple. All of this – the world, the plants and animals, the air we breathe, the water, the sunshine, the earth – it is all for us to learn to live and enjoy – righteously. People were designed and created to exist forever. Talk to a ninety year old man and he will tell you he still feels like he is only nineteen years old inside of himself. It is just that his dirt-suit, his body cannot keep up with his mind and his spirit the way it used to when he was younger. When the Lord breathed life into Adam, it changed everything. Man became a living soul! We are given a free will, to do as we please even if that means the destruction of ourselves and others. We have the capacity for moral greatness, and the tendency for despicable debauchery built right into our internal makeup.

Yet, without knowledge of the Holy One, we will never become all we can be. We are all created with a God hole in our spirit. We will forever attempt to fill that empty place inside of us with anything that we think will satisfy the urgent, incessant yearning for something more. We will fill it with food and drink to excess, with alcohol or drugs, with lust for things or people, with pride or a wide array of other things that will never satisfy us. We were made with a God hole in our spirit that only God can fill. That was and still is by His grand design.

When we die and leave this world – and, we certainly will do that too someday – we will not take any physical thing with us out of this world. We arrived naked and we will depart naked. Our name will fade away and our place will remember us no more.

Psalms 103:15 *As for* man, his days *are* as grass: as a flower of the field, so he flourisheth. 16 For the wind passeth over it, and it is gone; and the place thereof shall know it no more.

In my life, I have known a great number of people who wanted to leave a legacy or a name for themselves when they depart from this planet. In fact, I was one of them for the longest time. Searching for a way to make a name for yourself, so you can leave something of yourself for the world to remember is like chasing the wind. Mostly, it often has to do with great ideas or huge businesses that really do not mean very much in the long run. If it does not further the cause of God, or help people see Him in all His glory, it really is not worth anything. It is indeed hay and stubble, and it will not survive the purifying fire and glory of God.

1 Corinthians 3:11 For other foundation can no man lay than that is laid, which is Jesus Christ. 12 Now if any man build upon this foundation gold, silver, precious stones, wood, hay, stubble; 13 Every man's work shall be made manifest: for the day shall declare it, because it shall be revealed by fire; and the fire shall try every man's work of what sort it is.

What we should do is create a name for ourselves simply by how much we love others. "He loved his parents, his wife and family, and even his neighbor as he loved himself and he loved God."

Now, that is a legacy that will stand the test of time. Or, "he loved much and was loved much. He did not love his own life to the death, or he was not afraid to stand and die for what he thought was important." These are worthy of remembrance and will also stand the test of time.

Matthew 22:37 Jesus said unto him, Thou shalt love the Lord thy God with all thy heart, and with all thy soul, and with all thy mind. 38 This is the first and great commandment. 39 And the second *is* like unto it, Thou shalt love thy neighbour as thyself.

Life is all about people. It is not about the one with the most toys winning. Anything less than loving God with all your being and loving your neighbor as you love yourself is a life that is unworthy of our awesome Creator. Who is my neighbor? Every other person on this planet is my neighbor and I need to reach out to them and tell them that God loves them too. After all, he went to the cross and laid down His life for them just as much as He did it for me. One thing about the Billy Graham Evangelistic Association is their assertion that in regard to every person, God knows their name. That really hits me and strikes a chord with me. When I first read Franklin Grahams book about this (*The Name*), I was so moved it literally hung on me for days.

I have had other people tell me I should go easy, do not push people to decide about Jesus. If they are supposed to choose Him, they will in due time. Otherwise, it will just offend them and make you look weird. I have had others tell me that all roads lead to heaven. God is so good, He would never condemn someone for small sins. He will just forgive them and they will make it to heaven too, so do not get too excited about the gospel of Jesus Christ. Or, is not all religion the same? One road is as good as another isn't it? Why not allah, buddha or krishna? Are they not good too?

These are all lies and the people who spout them will someday wish they had told the truth. I am not wishing anything bad on them; really I am not, but I would hate to have to stand before

Jehovah Elohim Yahweh and describe why I told people buddha or allah were the same as He is. Our God is a consuming fire. He is Holy and righteous, and sin cannot exist in His presence – now or ever! He is immense! He holds the entire universe (not just the known universe) in the palm of His hand! He is a loving, merciful and kind God. But, He is righteous too. There will never be justice on this earth until He arrives and brings it with Him. He is justice and He will do all He said He would, no matter how many people want to tell us He is too soft or too gentle for that.

There are so many accounts in the bible of God exercising His wrath. He has warned us, over and over again. Do this or that, and I will have to do this. We cannot plead ignorance or pretend like we did not know, He knows us better than we know ourselves. He told Ezekiel if he did not warn the people he saw a sword coming, that He would hold Ezekiel responsible for their blood.

Ezekiel 33:4 Then whosoever heareth the sound of the trumpet, and taketh not warning; if the sword come, and take him away, his blood shall be upon his own head.

Ezekiel 33:6 But if the watchman see the sword come, and blow not the trumpet, and the people be not warned; if the sword come, and take *any* person from among them, he is taken away in his iniquity; but his blood will I require at the watchman's hand.

We are our brother's keeper. There is no way around that. If we love him, we will warn him. Whenever someone tells me they do not want to be too pushy about the gospel and just let things ride, I ask them if they really love their brother. For if they really love him, they will not let another day go by without making sure their brother knows the truth about Jesus. What if their brother leaves their presence and is killed in a car accident on the way home? Their brother might burn in hell forever because they did not want to be too pushy? Not me. God willing, I cannot and will not ever allow that to come to pass in my life ever again.

Hell is very real. Only the enemy, those who love this world and those in the camp of the enemy deny its existence! What is the best camouflage? Why, hide something in plain sight of course. All religions are manmade. God did not create all the religions of this world. Man did. Within Christianity, God did not create all the denominations – again, man did. All religions attempt to control the people and provide a framework for living together within a very specific set of rules of conduct and morality. Yet, even the absence of all rules and morality is a religion to some. Satan asks "did God really say?" Yes, in fact He did and we have that evidence in the Bible and it has been faithfully and miraculously preserved for us by God Himself.

There is only one God and He is existent in three persons – the Father, the Son and the Holy Spirit. Everything else the world tries to sell us as God is a lie and will cause us more harm than we can imagine. We must come to grips with that and not allow ourselves to be deceived by these lies. The Lord told us to worship no other gods before Him.

Acts 4:12 Neither is there salvation in any other: for there is none other name under heaven given among men, whereby we must be saved.

Jesus is the way, the light and the life. Jesus is about people and He is about us. We need to be about Him! We need to remain firm and strong and not cave into politically correct world views just because it seems like the nice thing to do. Elijah slew all four hundred and fifty of baal's prophets.

1 Kings 18:40 And Elijah said unto them, Take the prophets of Baal; let not one of them escape. And they took them: and Elijah brought them down to the brook Kishon, and slew them there.

Elijah would be branded as a radical terrorist or as a murderer in today's society for being too harsh, too simplistic and being downright cruel. But, he was none of these. He was God's man and that is what God wanted done. Remember, being nice to someone who wants to cut your throat will get your throat cut.

We simply cannot stand by and allow humanists, or any other worshipers of darkness dictate how we live or who we worship. We must stand up and be counted as people of the Word. We must stop compromising with sin, with political correctness or with wimpy responses to things we know are not right.

There is nothing in this world that compares to people. Absolutely nothing has as much value to God, or to His people. We must make every effort to reach all we can for the kingdom of God. Time is running out so we must be about His business!

Father, please teach us to truly love our neighbor as we love ourselves. Help us to reach out to the lost, the dying, and those bound for hell and tell them the good news about Jesus. Teach us to love with our hands and our hearts in Jesus name. Amen.

Virtue

"We need to set our sights high and refuse the traditions of men who say that it is impossible to do as Jesus instructed us." ~ John G. Lake

Philippians 4:8 Finally, brethren, whatsoever things are true, whatsoever things *are* honest, whatsoever things *are* just, whatsoever things *are* pure, whatsoever things *are* lovely, whatsoever things *are* of good report; if *there be* any virtue, and if *there be* any praise, think on these things.

2 Peter 1:3 According as his divine power hath given unto us all things that *pertain* unto life and godliness, through the knowledge of him that hath called us to glory and virtue:

Psalms 101:2 I will behave myself wisely in a perfect way. O when wilt thou come unto me? I will walk within my house with a perfect heart.

I love this last verse. I will walk in my house with a perfect heart! I will be honorable and righteous when no one is looking! That is character and integrity! What a beautiful picture! When no one is watching, and I am all alone, I will still walk in purity. It is easier to be holy and righteous when we know others are looking, or watching us. We can measure up then with no problem at all. But the real question is when we are all alone, and no one is watching, can we still be holy?

Just what is virtue? According to the dictionary virtue means moral excellence. A virtue is a positive trait or quality subjectively deemed to be morally excellent and thus is valued as a foundation of principle and good moral being. Personal virtues are characteristics valued as promoting individual and collective wellbeing. The opposite of virtue is vice.

One of the problems of modern society is that we have turned away from what is right, what is just and what is morally correct. We have allowed barbarians to come and dictate what is acceptable to us as a society. In today's America, everything is ok and nothing is taboo except doing right and having high moral standards! We have indeed fallen far from where we once stood. The verses in the bible that speak to me about this are:

Isaiah 5:20 Woe unto them that call evil good, and good evil; that put darkness for light, and light for darkness; that put bitter for sweet, and sweet for bitter!

Isaiah 59:14 And judgment is turned away backward, and justice standeth afar off: for truth is fallen in the street, and equity cannot enter.

Lamentations 5:16 The crown is fallen *from* our head: woe unto us, that we have sinned!

Hosea 14:1 O Israel, return unto the LORD thy God; for thou hast fallen by thine iniquity.

Revelation 18:2 And he cried mightily with a strong voice, saying, Babylon the great is fallen, is fallen, and is become the habitation of devils, and the hold of every foul spirit, and a cage of every unclean and hateful bird.

As a people, we must turn back to our origins. We were formed as one nation under God, following and enforcing Judeo-Christian values in our society, in our homes, in our schools and in our courts. Our moral turpitude has caused us to come to the place we now inhabit. The only way back is to change our mind (repent), and listen to the truth once again and follow those same precepts we once held dear.

The picture that comes to my mind is of Nehemiah rebuilding the wall of Jerusalem. We each need to take our place working on that wall. Our place is where we are right now. We need to take a stand where we are and rebuild the section of the wall in front of us.

There will be great opposition but we will persevere if we stay focused. We have to work with a tool in one hand and a weapon in the other just as the people of Jerusalem did in Nehemiah's day.

Our wall is not a physical wall, but a spiritual wall. We need to declare the truth and stand for the truth, and not accept compromise or defeat. The stakes are too high. The Lord told us:

2 Chronicles 7:14 If my people, which are called by my name, shall humble themselves, and pray, and seek my face, and turn from their wicked ways; then will I hear from heaven, and will forgive their sin, and will heal their land.

We cannot repair another's section of this wall; just our own. "If my people", means us, we Christians. God did not say we had to convince everyone in this country, or take over the courts or elect the right candidates. He said, if my people will humble themselves and pray, then I will hear from heaven, forgive them and heal their land. Praise God! It is not our strength, it is His.

The Lord is returning for a pure bride, not one soiled with lust, greed or pride. We must refrain from all evil, even from the appearance of evil in every aspect of our lives. We must live and display to all those around us moral excellence, goodness and righteousness. We cannot compromise with sin in any way. I cannot do this for my neighbor, but I can do it for my family, and my neighborhood. I cannot pluck the splinter from my neighbor's eye until I remove the plank from my own eye!

Matthew 7:3 And why beholdest thou the mote that is in thy brother's eye, but considerest not the beam that is in thine own eye? 4 Or how wilt thou say to thy brother, Let me pull out the mote out of thine eye; and, behold, a beam *is* in thine own eye?

In *"developing a Supernatural Lifestyle, a Practical Guide,"* by Kris Vallotton, on page 74 and 75 of his book, I found a list of virtues to live by. These are amazing and really describe how I want my children to live. As we look in the mirror, who or what do we see? Here are a few we need to add to our own repertoire:

- We will serve God first and honor Him always, both in life and death.
- We will be honest, loyal, trustworthy, and men of our word, no matter what the price.
- We will be Men of the Word, believing and standing on every Word that proceeds from the mouth of God.
- We will keep our values, no matter how much they cost us, and if we fail, we will be quick to repent.

Lord Jesus, please help me to be holy, pure in my thoughts and reasoning, and more righteous in my actions! As the scripture says, you have made us into a peculiar people, a holy nation, a royal priesthood. Through the power and enabling of Your Spirit within, please help me to be all that you intended me to be. Help me tear down all the idols of today's culture that so easily find a place in me and help me rid myself of everything that defiles me. In Jesus' name I pray, Amen.

The Anointing

Exodus 29:7 Then shalt thou take the anointing oil, and pour *it* upon his head, and anoint him.

"The Holy Ghost does not come upon methods, but upon men. He does not anoint machinery, but men. He does not work through organizations, but through men. He does not dwell in buildings, but men. He indwells the Body of Christ, directs its activities, distributes its forces, and empowers its members." ~ Samuel Chadwick

1 John 2:27 But the anointing which ye have received of him abideth in you, and ye need not that any man teach you: but as the same anointing teacheth you of all things, and is truth, and is no lie, and even as it hath taught you, ye shall abide in him.

1 John 2:20 But ye have an unction from the Holy One, and ye know all things.

What is the Anointing?

"The anointing is not some mystical something out there. The anointing is the presence and power of God manifested." ~ Rodney Howard-Browne

The anointing of God is so vitally important to understand that I will go into its description in some detail. Please consider the messianic prophesy of Isaiah:

Isaiah 61:1 The Spirit of the Lord GOD is upon me; because the LORD hath anointed me to preach good tidings unto the meek; he hath sent me to bind up the brokenhearted, to proclaim liberty to the captives, and the opening of the prison to them that are bound;

The Lord anointed, proclaimed and sent Jesus! Of course, Jesus is the only person who fulfills this verse. He is the Messiah! He is the only person who ever lived who fulfilled every prophesy foretelling of His advent.

The word "Messiah" (mashiach) comes from the verb mashach, which means to smear or anoint with oil, usually for the purpose of dedicating or consecrating something, such as a temple vessel or someone for the service of God. The person, or thing anointed by God was called mashiach, an anointed one or chosen one. Thus, mashiach is an anointed or consecrated person or thing.

In simple terms, the anointing is the presence of the Holy Spirit being smeared upon someone. It is the overflowing life of Jesus which imparts supernatural ability and strength enabling an individual to perform a special task or function in an office he is called and appointed to. In a spiritual sense, a person who is anointed has the power of God on him. The anointing of the Holy Spirit enables a person to do what they cannot do in their own strength. Anointing, as described in the Bible, can be defined as: "God on flesh doing those things that flesh cannot do."

Another thing we need to understand about the anointing is that it is holy and it must be treated with respect. The anointing is available twenty-four hours a day, seven days a week. When the anointing is in operation, it manifests with a divine purpose.

In ancient times, God anointed people to function in a particular office. There were three offices people were anointed for: the office of a priest, the office of a prophet and the office of a king. The significance of the divine anointing involves:

- Separation of that person for service to God
- God's inviolable choice of the anointed one
- God's favor that accompanies the anointing

Jesus' name is Jesus of Nazareth. His title is Christ which means the Anointed One. You hear people refer to Jesus Christ as if Christ was His last name, but it is not. It is His title, the Anointed One of God – the Mashiach. Christ comes from the Greek word Cristos, which is a translation of the Hebrew Meshiach, or as we say in English "Messiah." Jesus was anointed by God beyond measure.

John 3:34 For he whom God hath sent speaketh the words of God: for God giveth not the Spirit by measure unto him.

When Jesus was anointed, no oil was used as a symbolic presence of the Holy Spirit. Instead, the Holy Spirit himself appeared in the form of a dove, descended and remained on Jesus. There at the Jordan River, Jesus became what the prophets said He would be - Meshiach, Cristos - the anointed one, called, appointed and sent by God.

Luke 3:21 Now when all the people were baptized, it came to pass, that Jesus also being baptized, and praying, the heaven was opened, 22 And the Holy Ghost descended in a bodily shape like a dove upon him, and a voice came from heaven, which said, Thou art my beloved Son; in thee I am well pleased.

The key element is that God the Father calls Jesus, and God the

Holy Spirit empowers Jesus. And then, as we see in Luke 4 with Jesus' initial sermon in the synagogue, God the Son, Jesus the Anointed One, begins to declare who He is and live out his calling. Now, in Jesus' own words, here is what that anointing meant:

Luke 4:14 And Jesus returned in the power of the Spirit into Galilee: and there went out a fame of him through all the region round about. 15 And he taught in their synagogues, being glorified of all. 16 And he came to Nazareth, where he had been brought up: and, as his custom was, he went into the synagogue on the sabbath day, and stood up for to read. 17 And there was delivered unto him the book of the prophet Esaias. And when he had opened the book, he found the place where it was written, 18 The Spirit of the Lord is upon me, because he hath anointed me to preach the gospel to the poor; he hath sent me to heal the brokenhearted, to preach deliverance to the captives, and recovering of sight to the blind, to set at liberty them that are bruised, 19 To preach the acceptable year of the Lord. 20 And he closed the book, and he gave it again to the minister, and sat down. And the eyes of all them that were in the synagogue were fastened on him. 21 And he began to say unto them, This day is this scripture fulfilled in your ears.

What was Jesus the Anointed One so uniquely anointed for? He was to take up in Himself the perfection and fulfillment of all the special offices that God had used for centuries to guide and lead His people. This means we go back to the Old Testament and see that God directed and connected with the lives of his people primarily through the three offices mentioned earlier:

- priest - mediator between God and people
- prophet - God's spokesperson
- king - God's ruler over his people

Now these three – priest, prophet and king - come together in a perfectly fulfilling way in Jesus as God's perfect priest, chief prophet and eternal king.

Jesus as Priest

The bible reveals that God the Father called Jesus, and God the Spirit anointed Jesus to the office of Priest, our only high priest.

Hebrews 7:17 For he testifieth, Thou art a priest for ever after the order of Melchisedec.

Hebrews 7:20-21 And inasmuch as not without an oath he was made priest: 21 (For those priests were made without an oath; but this with an oath by him that said unto him, The Lord sware and will not repent, Thou art a priest for ever after the order of Melchisedec:)

Hebrews 7:24 But this man, because he continueth ever, hath an unchangeable priesthood. 25 Wherefore he is able also to save them to the uttermost that come unto God by him, seeing he ever liveth to make intercession for them. 26 For such an high priest became us, who is holy, harmless, undefiled, separate from sinners, and made higher than the heavens; 27 Who needeth not daily, as those high priests, to offer up sacrifice, first for his own sins, and then for the people's: for this he did once, when he offered up himself.

Jesus lives to ever make intercession for us! How awesome! The enemy accuses us constantly, but we have the Lord standing there making intercession for us.

Jesus as Prophet

The prophet speaks the Word of God to His people. Jesus is the great prophet. In fact, He is so great that He is called, in John 1, not merely the one that speaks the Word of God. He IS the Word.

John 1:1 In the beginning was the Word, and the Word was with God, and the Word was God.

God Almighty Himself tells us to listen to Him:

Matthew 17:5 While he yet spake, behold, a bright cloud overshadowed them: and behold a voice out of the cloud, which said, This is my beloved Son, in whom I am well pleased; hear ye him.

We are told that the testimony of Jesus is the spirit of prophecy:

Revelation 19:10 And I fell at his feet to worship him. And he said unto me, See thou do it not: I am thy fellowservant, and of thy brethren that have the testimony of Jesus: worship God: for the testimony of Jesus is the spirit of prophecy.

Jesus as King

Jesus the Anointed One who is our master, our teacher, our savior, and also our king.

John 18:36 Jesus answered, My kingdom is not of this world: if my kingdom were of this world, then would my servants fight, that I should not be delivered to the Jews: but now is my kingdom not from hence. 37 Pilate therefore said unto him, Art thou a king then? Jesus answered, Thou sayest that I am a king. To this end was I born, and for this cause came I into the world, that I should bear witness unto the truth. Every one that is of the truth heareth my voice.

So, Jesus is shown to be all of these things to us: Jesus, the King; my king, your king; Jesus, the priest; my priest, your priest; Jesus, the prophet; my prophet, your prophet; Jesus, the Word of God, the way to God and the rule of God.

Moreover, if we are in Christ, or in the anointed one, then we share in his anointing. The name we bear, Christians, means little anointed ones in honor of our King. Indeed, if Christ be in us, then His anointing resides in and on us as well. This anointing is for service to God and is affected by how we live our lives.

1 John 2:27 But the anointing which ye have received of him abideth in you, and ye need not that any man teach you: but as the same anointing teacheth you of all things, and is truth, and is no lie, and even as it hath taught you, ye shall abide in him.

Father, please help us understand your anointing so we can flow in it at all times. Prepare us for a greater measure of your anointing in Jesus name I pray. Amen.

Understanding the Anointing

"Love not the world, neither the things that are in the world. You have an anointing from the Holy One: live by it! Give yourself to God; live for him wholly and utterly; see to it that, where you personally are concerned, the things of this world are scored off satan's books and transferred to God's account." ~ Watchman Nee

The first thing we have to recognize is that God anoints His people for a purpose! He anointed Jesus, and he anoints His children. Why? Look closely at this scripture:

Acts 10:38 How God anointed Jesus of Nazareth with the Holy Ghost and with power: who went about doing good, and healing all that were oppressed of the devil; for God was with him.

Notice it does not say: "How God anointed Jesus the Son of God with the Holy Ghost...." What it says is that God anointed Jesus of Nazareth; Jesus the man. You see, what so many Christians do not understand is that even though Jesus was the only begotten Son of God, He left all of His power and glory in Heaven and came to earth in the same form as every other man.

Philippians 2:8 And being found in fashion as a man, he humbled himself, and became obedient unto death, even the death of the cross.

Hebrews 2:17 Wherefore in all things it behooved him to be made like unto his brethren, that he might be a merciful and faithful high priest in things pertaining to God, to make reconciliation for the sins of the people.

- He was born a man
- He lived on earth as a man
- As a man He had no more power than you or I
- He hungered and thirsted as a man
- He was tempted as other men are tempted

- He suffered as a man
- He died as a man

The anointing of God brings God's power to whoever is anointed. It is extremely important we understand that in the Gospels, Jesus never performed any miracles until after He was anointed by the Holy Spirit; therefor it was only after the Spirit of God in the form of the Holy Ghost, descended on Him that he began His ministry. Regardless of what many people think, there is no biblical evidence that Jesus performed any miracles, nor did he enter into ministry until after He received the Holy Spirit.

It is also important that Jesus told the disciples not to go anywhere or do anything, not even to witness to others until they had received the anointing or baptism of the Holy Ghost.

Luke 24:49 And, behold, I send the promise of my Father upon you: but tarry ye in the city of Jerusalem, until ye be endued with power from on high.

We are anointed by God. The most important thing for us to understand is that every born-again child of God has received the Spirit of God and thus an anointing of the Spirit. Every born-again child of God has received the indwelling of the Holy Spirit. This is not to be confused with the infilling or the baptism of the Holy Spirit which is a completely separate experience, but every born-again believer has received the Spirit of God.

Acts 1:8 But ye shall receive power, after that the Holy Ghost is come upon you: and ye shall be witnesses unto me both in Jerusalem, and in all Judaea, and in Samaria, and unto the uttermost part of the earth.

1 Corinthians 2:12 Now we have received, not the spirit of the world, but the spirit which is of God; that we might know the things that are freely given to us of God.

Romans 8:15 For ye have not received the spirit of bondage again to fear; but ye have received the Spirit of adoption, whereby we cry, Abba, Father.

Ephesians 1:13 In whom ye also trusted, after that ye heard the word of truth, the gospel of your salvation: in whom also after that ye believed, ye were sealed with that holy Spirit of promise,

There are different types of anointing as well as different degrees of anointing. Jesus was anointed beyond measure. Samson and Joshua possessed a warrior anointing. Aaron possessed a priestly anointing. David was both a king and a warrior but possessed all three types of anointing. There is an anointing for administration, healing, worship and intercession. Jesus told us we can do nothing without Him. The deeper in God we go, the deeper and richer the anointing becomes. The anointing often comes upon us when it is needed because we could not stand to walk in constant anointing as it would wear us out. There are some who walk in very anointed ways most of their lives, but not many.

As I said there are many different types of individual anointing: the five fold ministry; special anointings of the gifts of the Spirit; special anointings in the area of helps, administrations, etc; and, an individual anointing.

The fivefold ministry (Apostle, Prophet, Evangelist, Pastor, Teacher) is referenced here:

Ephesians 4:11 And he gave some, apostles; and some, prophets; and some, evangelists; and some, pastors and teachers;

When God calls someone into the fivefold ministry He anoints them with supernatural power and ability to carry out the functions of that office. When we understand this, it is easier to recognize those who are called and anointed by God for the office they stand in, because they seem to have a supernatural ability to carry out the functions of that office with ease and excellence.

It is also easier to recognize when someone is not called and anointed to an office because they are not able to perform the duties of that office in a manner consistent with the excellence required by the Lord for that office. Everything seems to be a struggle for them, and the enemy is constantly able to overcome them and their goals.

It is important to mention here that no one should ever attempt to stand in a ministry office without the call of God and the anointing that comes with the office. Not only is it dangerous for the individual personally to attempt to stand in one of the fivefold ministry offices if they have not been called and anointed to that office, but it can also bring great harm to the body of Christ.

The special anointing of the gifts of the Spirit is mentioned in these verses:

1 Corinthians 12:7 But the manifestation of the Spirit is given to every man to profit withal. 8 For to one is given by the Spirit the word of wisdom; to another the word of knowledge by the same Spirit; 9 To another faith by the same Spirit; to another the gifts of healing by the same Spirit; 10 To another the working of miracles; to another prophecy; to another discerning of spirits; to another divers kinds of tongues; to another the interpretation of tongues:

11 But all these worketh that one and the selfsame Spirit, dividing to every man severally as he will.

And, the special anointing in the area of helps, administrations and such are mentioned here in scripture:

1 Corinthians 12:28 And God hath set some in the church, first apostles, secondarily prophets, thirdly teachers, after that miracles, then gifts of healings, helps, governments, diversities of tongues.

The Lord does grant special anointing to certain individuals who seem to be able to operate in a higher degree of various gifts. I have seen, and known people who operate in a higher degree of the gifts of healing than most other people, and still others where the Word of Knowledge is in manifestation to a greater degree than in others. This special anointing is granted by the Lord for whatever reason He chooses and is not something that anyone can simply call upon at their own discretion for it is as the Spirit wills.

1 Corinthians 12:11 But all these worketh that one and the selfsame Spirit, dividing to every man severally as he will.

Additionally, every born-again person is anointed to some degree to be a help to the body of Christ and to assist in the many different needs of the ministry as they are needed and called upon by the pastor and other leaders of the church.

Finally, there is an individual anointing.

1 John 2:20 But ye have an unction from the Holy One, and ye know all things.

1 John 2:27 But the anointing which ye have received of him abideth in you, and ye need not that any man teach you: but as the same anointing teacheth you of all things, and is truth, and is no lie, and even as it hath taught you, ye shall abide in him.

1 John 4:4 Ye are of God, little children, and have overcome them: because greater is he that is in you, than he that is in the world.

Now, notice three things:

- You have an anointing
- The anointing abides or lives in you
- The anointing is there for a purpose - to over-come the world

There is no doubt that we have an anointing because the Word of God says so: "But you have an unction (anointing) from the Holy One...." And, we see from the Scripture that this anointing or unction is not just a passive thing that is simply placed in us for some future unknown reason or just to simply seal us - but rather the anointing abides in us. The Greek Word used here that is translated as abides is "meno." It literally means to dwell, or take up residence and to remain and live.

This anointing is a living and tangible force that lives in us, it takes up residence in us and dwells in us, and best of all it remains in us and never leaves us! The reason for this is because we are talking about the Holy Spirit Himself, whom God has promised will come to live in us and will never leave nor forsake us.

2 Corinthians 6:16 And what agreement hath the temple of God with idols? for ye are the temple of the living God; as God hath said, I will dwell in them, and walk in them; and I will be their God, and they shall be my people.

John 14:16 And I will pray the Father, and he shall give you another Comforter, that he may abide with you for ever;

Hebrews 13:5 Let your conversation be without covetousness; and be content with such things as ye have: for he hath said, I will never leave thee, nor forsake thee.

Finally, the anointing that we have received of Him is for a purpose!

Acts 1:8 But ye shall receive power, after that the Holy Ghost is come upon you: and ye shall be witnesses unto me both in Jerusalem, and in all Judaea, and in Samaria, and unto the uttermost part of the earth.

1 John 4:4 Ye are of God, little children, and have overcome them: because greater is he that is in you, than he that is in the world.

According to scripture the purpose of the anointing is two-fold:

- To be a witness to the saving power and goodness of Christ
- To overcome the world and the things that are in it

The anointing confers the power to witness. The disciples received specific instructions from the Lord Jesus Himself that they were to wait in Jerusalem until they had been endued with power from on high. They were told not to go anywhere or do anything until they received this power or anointing of the Holy Ghost.

And, the anointing confers the power to overcome. The anointing that abides in us is there to help us to overcome those things that come against us and the plan of God for our lives. Such things as sickness, poverty, lack, weakness, doubt, anxiety, stress, confusion, depression, oppression, etc; all of which are tools the enemy uses against us.

Ephesians 5:18 And be not drunk with wine, wherein is excess; but be filled with the Spirit;

A careful study of the above scripture shows that the literal translation of the original Greek is as follows: "And be not drunk with wine, wherein is excess; but be being continually filled with the Spirit;"

Did you notice that we are to be continually filled? This would indicate that just being filled once is not enough! We must leak. Apparently the possibility exists that just like a battery, as we use the power or anointing, and as it flows out of us while ministering to others that we are literally drained to some degree and so we need to refill it. Otherwise, why would we need to be continually filled?

Father, fill us beyond measure with your Holy Spirit. Grant us wisdom and understanding about the anointing and how to walk in it and flow in it in accordance with your purposes and your will for our lives in Jesus name. Amen.

Corporate Anointing

"One hundred religious persons knit into a unity by careful organization do not constitute a church any more than eleven dead men make a football team." ~ A.W. Tozer

In the simplest terms, a corporate anointing is what happens when more than one believer is gathered together in the same place at the same time, and there is a singleness of purpose between them. Scripture indicates that not only is this somewhat different from the individual anointing in the sense that it affects more than that one person - but also that the corporate anointing is one of greater power. There is a concept of perfect unity where all those gathered are in one accord and of a single mind and purpose.

2 Chronicles 5:12 Also the Levites which were the singers, all of them of Asaph, of Heman, of Jeduthun, with their sons and their brethren, being arrayed in white linen, having cymbals and psalteries and harps, stood at the east end of the altar, and with them an hundred and twenty priests sounding with trumpets: 13 It came even to pass, as the trumpeters and singers were as one, to make one sound to be heard in praising and thanking the LORD; and when they lifted up their voice with the trumpets and cymbals and instruments of music, and praised the LORD, saying, For he is good; for his mercy endureth for ever: that then the house was filled with a cloud, even the house of the LORD; 14 So that the priests could not stand to minister by reason of the cloud: for the glory of the LORD had filled the house of God.

Notice in the above passage, that the first key we see is that all of the priests (120 of them) are in the same place at the same time, and just as important, they are acting as one and making one sound. They are in unison and in perfect agreement as to their purpose and intent.

There were not some who were praying or singing about one thing while others were praying and singing about something else. Nor

Corporate Anointing

were some off in another place while others were gathered together here. They were all in one place. They were all doing the same thing. They all had the same purpose and were acting as one. They were in perfect harmony and unity.

Now notice the similarity in these passages in Acts with those from 2 Chronicles:

Acts 2:1 And when the day of Pentecost was fully come, they were all with one accord in one place. 2 And suddenly there came a sound from heaven as of a rushing mighty wind, and it filled all the house where they were sitting. 3 And there appeared unto them cloven tongues like as of fire, and it sat upon each of them. 4 And they were all filled with the Holy Ghost, and began to speak with other tongues, as the Spirit gave them utterance.

Now, here is that same number again, one hundred and twenty:

Acts 1:15 And in those days Peter stood up in the midst of the disciples, and said, (the number of names together were about an hundred and twenty,)

And, again, they were united and lifted their voices in one accord:

Acts 4:24 And when they heard that, they lifted up their voice to God with one accord, and said, Lord, thou art God, which hast made heaven, and earth, and the sea, and all that in them is: 25 Who by the mouth of thy servant David hast said, Why did the heathen rage, and the people imagine vain things? 26 The kings of the earth stood up, and the rulers were gathered together against the Lord, and against his Christ. 27 For of a truth against thy holy child Jesus, whom thou hast anointed, both Herod, and Pontius Pilate, with the Gentiles, and the people of Israel, were gathered together, 28 For to do whatsoever thy hand and thy counsel determined before to be done. 29 And now, Lord, behold their threatenings: and grant unto thy servants, that with all boldness they may speak thy word, 30 By stretching forth thine hand to heal; and that signs and wonders may be done by the name of thy holy child Jesus. 31 And when they had prayed, the place was shaken where they were assembled together; and they were all filled with the Holy Ghost, and they spake the word of God with boldness.

Notice that like the account given to us in Chronicles, in both of these instances the people were all in one place - and they were acting in one accord, with one purpose and intent. Also notice that in each of these cases when there was a gathering of believers together acting corporately as one, that great power was released.

The Temple of God was filled with the Glory of God so much so, that the priests could not even stand up to minister [2 Chronicles 5:14]. There was a sound like a might rushing wind and the fire of God appeared and those present were all filled with the Holy Ghost and began to speak in tongues as the Spirit gave them utterance [Acts:2:1-4]. The place was shaken (the whole building shook) because of the power that was released [Acts 4:31]! These are demonstrations of God's awesome power!

Even a small gathering of believers who are together in one place and acting together with singleness of purpose can generate a release of this awesome power!

Acts 16:25 And at midnight Paul and Silas prayed, and sang praises unto God: and the prisoners heard them. 26 And suddenly there was a great earthquake, so that the foundations of the prison were shaken: and immediately all the doors were opened, and every one's bands were loosed.

Here we have two believers assembled together in one place and singing and praising God together as one, and it resulted in such a release of the power of God that it caused an earthquake that shook the very foundations of the prison! And, even more noteworthy is the fact that not only were Paul and Silas freed, but ALL of the prisoners had their shackles thrown off!

Isaiah 10:27 And it shall come to pass in that day, that his burden shall be taken away from off thy shoulder, and his yoke from off thy neck, and the yoke shall be destroyed because of the anointing.

This anointing is an order of magnitude greater by the number of those who are gathered. If one will chase a thousand and two ten thousand, how many will one hundred chase?

Deuteronomy 32:30 How should one chase a thousand, and two put ten thousand to flight, except their Rock had sold them, and the LORD had shut them up?

The corporate anointing is so powerful that it can affect not only you, but everyone in the vicinity! That is what makes our assembling together so important. Can you see now why it is so important that we as believers come together regularly as the Word of God instructs us to? You see, there are some things that can only be accomplished when the people of God assemble together as one.

Hebrews 10:25 Not forsaking the assembling of ourselves together, as the manner of some is; but exhorting one another: and so much the more, as ye see the day approaching.

I have personally seen manifestations of incredible power and miracles when believers are assembled together in one place. Nowhere in the Word of God are we told to forsake being a part of a local body - no matter what the justification is. Christians are instructed by the Lord to be part of a local body and to come together regularly and often in one place to pray, to worship God, and to be taught the Word of God.

Christian television is great, and online ministries are a great resource for fellowship and growth as books, tapes and CD's are awesome tools of learning. But none of these produce the results that can be manifested when believers assemble together in one place and come into agreement with one purpose, even if it is simply singing and praying together. Imagine what a large gathering for prayer and intercession can accomplish!

I have seen people healed miraculously and instantaneously just by being in a gathering of believers who were singing and praising God! No hands were laid on them and no prayers were offered for them. My wife enters into worship faster than anyone I have ever seen, and I have seen her succumb to the Spirit in corporate worship as soon as we enter the sanctuary and remain so for hours. It is because of the release of power that comes when there is a corporate anointing, and the Word of God shows us example after example of how the corporate anointing is far greater than that of the individual anointing.

Awesome Father, please help us understand how powerful we are when we walk together in love and unity. Teach us to come into one accord that your will may be done on earth as it is in heaven. In the name that is above all other names, Jesus I pray. Amen.

Communion with the Holy Spirit

"Whenever we find the presence of the Holy Spirit, we will always find the supernatural." ~ Kathryn Kuhlman

We must not live our lives like the rest of the world, or the anointing within us will ebb and flow away from us. You see, there is a cost to the anointing of God. The price is our heart. We are to seek God with all our heart just as we are commanded in Jeremiah:

Jeremiah 29:13 And ye shall seek me, and find me, when ye shall search for me with all your heart.

If we obey this scripture, the anointing upon our lives and our ministries will increase and become clearer and more distinct. As we learn to walk as holy vessels of the Lord, the anointing upon us will become purer as well. We need to learn how to live in the flow of the anointing:

- Learn to recognize the presence of the Holy Spirit
- Learn to be open to the guidance of the Holy Spirit
- Learn to give the Holy Spirit the freedom to lead our lives and meetings
- Learn to understand and recognize which attributes of the anointing of the Holy Spirit are present
- Learn to partner with the Holy Spirit
- Learn to be taught by the Holy Spirit
- Learn to enter into an intimate relationship with the Holy Spirit
- Learn to honor and steward the anointing of the Holy Spirit
- Learn to understand the differences of the anointing's of the Holy Spirit and work in harmony with Him to manifest Christ's Kingdom

The Holy Spirit is ready, willing and able to teach us this Himself. The key to this is to position ourselves to hear His voice and learn from Him. Some have treated the Holy Spirit like some kind of exotic wild animal or pet. Others have tried to keep the Holy Ghost caged up fearing that He may get out of hand. Their thinking goes something like this: He is fascinating to talk about or to look at, and even to read about in the scriptures, but we do not want to get too close to Him. We do not want to let Him "loose" in our churches.

The truth is that most of us are fearful of the power of the Holy Spirit because we do not know Him. We have an Old Testament mindset. The anointing of the Holy Spirit still terrifies us. In recent history, the men and women who have been used the most powerfully by God are those who have overcome their fear of the unknown and fear of the supernatural and boldly entered into a intimate relationship with the third member of the God Head - the Holy Ghost!

I believe that fellowship with the Holy Spirit is the most important key to understanding the anointing of the Holy Spirit, and to position ourselves to receive and increase the anointing of the Holy Spirit.

The Holy Spirit wants to be our friend! The tragedy is that we have allowed religious traditions, and fears of the supernatural to bring the power of the Holy Spirit to naught in many of our churches and lives. Imagine if you will that the God of the universe desires to have a deep and intimate relationship with you and I. He wants to be our friend and to live with us at all times. The Holy Spirit wants us to walk with Him every day. He wants to share every second of our lives with us. He wants to guide us and lead us in every aspect of our lives, even in the most seemingly insignificant details. Yet, for most of us that is just too great a cost. We want our freedom. We like our independence, but we also want to have the anointing and power of God. So, we are torn between wanting all of God and losing personal control over our own lives.

2 Corinthians 13:14 The grace of the Lord Jesus Christ, and the love of God, and the communion of the Holy Ghost, be with you all. Amen.

Communion with the Holy Spirit

The above scripture illustrates this spiritual dynamic; The grace of the Lord Jesus Christ, and the love of God, and the communion of the Holy Spirit be with you all. The concept put forth by the last passage is that of koinonia, or communion by intimate participation. The word used here for communion is not speaking about the communion table or the Lord's Supper. This is speaking of a personal relationship with God and other Christians. This is a call to an intimate and private relationship with the person of the Holy Spirit.

It is our responsibility once we receive the anointing to cherish, maintain and steward it. Even as I am writing this passage the Holy Spirit is whispering to me. Some of you reading this will begin to grow in the power of God and the anointing's of the Holy Spirit as you put these principles into practice in your lives and ministries. Remember to honor and steward the anointing. Remember to place your relationship with God first.

The anointing of the Holy Spirit is tangible; it is active and it is alive. The anointing of the Holy Spirit is also transferable; one might say that it is contagious, infectious, catching, communicable, and transmittable. I believe that the anointing of the Holy Spirit can be imparted from one person to another. However, if the one receiving the anointing does not steward it with intimacy and friendship with God, then just like a flighty dove the anointing will leave. There is a cost to the anointing and the price is our heart.

I pray that you catch onto this and it starts a fire in your life, in your ministry and in your city, and spreads throughout your nation leading to wholesale salvations and revival! Here are nine points to consider about the anointing of the Holy Spirit.

1. The anointing of the Holy Spirit is tangible. You can feel Him. Praise and worship enhance our ability to enter in.

2. The anointing of the Holy Spirit is transferable. You can have it. Jesus secured it for us.

3. The anointing of the Holy Spirit will glorify Jesus and testify of Him. Jesus taught us this aspect of the anointing of the Holy Spirit:

John 15:26 But when the Comforter is come, whom I will send unto you from the Father, even the Spirit of truth, which proceedeth from the Father, he shall testify of me:

4. The anointing of the Holy Spirit varies in subtle ways. We can learn these minute variations and learn to work with God in symphony because the Holy Spirit will teach us how to accomplish this Himself! We need to ask God for wisdom. He has promised to give wisdom to us all liberally and without reproach.

James 1:5 If any of you lack wisdom, let him ask of God, that giveth to all men liberally, and upbraideth not; and it shall be given him.

5. We need to be in an intimate and personal relationship with the Holy Spirit. We need communion or koinonia with God. When we learn about communion and grow in wisdom and stature with God we will begin to recognize the subtle ways that the Holy Spirit is "flowing" or working and then "co-labor" with Him in harmony and manifest Christ's Kingdom in our sphere of influence.

6. The anointing of the Holy Spirit manifests in a variety of ways. We find the anointing of the Holy Spirit is upon individuals and often released to minister in five basic ways:

Ephesians 4:11 And he gave some, apostles; and some, prophets; and some, evangelists; and some, pastors and teachers; 12 For the perfecting of the saints, for the work of the ministry, for the edifying of the body of Christ: 13 Till we all come in the unity of the faith, and of the knowledge of the Son of God, unto a perfect man, unto the measure of the stature of the fulness of Christ:

Let me add that a person may minister in the five anointings of the Holy Spirit listed above without actually holding a ministry office.

7. We need to honor and understand how to steward or guard the

anointing of the Holy Spirit. He is precious and so is His anointing. The Holy Spirit really is a lot like a dove. If we grieve Him, He will fly away just like a dove. I do not know how many times I have been in meetings where the Holy Spirit settles and begins to manifest and then someone stops His anointing from fully manifesting by stepping out of His flow. Often, that person is not even aware of the fact that they missed what the anointing of the Holy Spirit was seeking to do. They just have an agenda to follow and do not allow or do not recognize that the Holy Spirit has a different and often better plan.

This understanding of stewarding the Holy Spirit can take time and can be a learning curve. But we need to realize there is a flow and rhythm, and seek to move in obedience to His wishes at all times.

8. It is very important that we understand the dispensation of the times in which we live. We are living in a God ordained moment of time in which the anointing of the Holy Spirit is available to everyone. His anointing is not just for "chosen vessels" any more. You can have the anointing of the Holy Spirit. It is available to all born again believers.

9. The anointing of the Holy Spirit is critical for the hour in which we live. Understanding the anointing of the Holy Spirit, and how to walk in harmony with the anointing of the Holy Spirit may very well save your life in the coming days.

Father, please ignite the fires within us so that we burn ever brighter for you and for the kingdom of God! I pray for eyes to see and ears to hear what the Spirit is doing and saying. Teach us how to discern and respond to the unction of the Holy Spirit and teach us neither to grieve Him nor to quench Him in any way. Please teach us how to obey His unction in all love and humility, in Jesus name. Amen.

The Flow of the Holy Spirit

"It is not your ability, it is Gods ability flowing through you." ~ Benny Hinn

John 7:37 In the last day, that great day of the feast, Jesus stood and cried, saying, If any man thirst, let him come unto me, and drink. 38 He that believeth on me, as the scripture hath said, out of his belly shall flow rivers of living water. 39 (But this spake he of the Spirit, which they that believe on him should receive: for the Holy Ghost was not yet given; because that Jesus was not yet glorified.)

Water is one of the symbols of the Holy Spirit. Here we see Jesus speaking of "flowing rivers," but he is not just talking about natural water and natural rivers. Jesus says that the rivers He is referring to flow out of the heart of those who believe in Him. This passage leaves no doubt about what is being referred to as verse 39 clearly tells us that this is speaking of the Holy Spirit.

Jesus shows us that there are important truths we can learn about the Holy Spirit and His ministry through us by comparing the Holy Spirit in operation to the flow of a river. If we can understand this aspect of the Holy Spirit's ministry and operation through us, we can learn to "flow" with Him. Just like rivers flow, so the Holy Spirit flows too. You may have heard terms like, "the move of the Holy Spirit" or "the flow of the Spirit." Flow can be defined as: to move freely from one place to another in a steady unbroken stream; unhindered steady movement.

The important point here is that a river is not static. When something flows it moves. When water becomes static, it is no longer a river, but instead it is now a dam, a lake or a pond. Rivers move, and in the same way there is a "flow" or a "move" of the Spirit of God. Unfortunately, in many churches, movement has disappeared and things have become static. Some people try to keep the church stuck at a particular place and get upset when there is any movement. If we are going to stay close to God, individually or as a church, we need to keep up or stay in step with the movement of the Holy Spirit. Without movement, the church becomes lifeless and static; resulting in it becoming irrelevant and stale very much like water that becomes static begins to stagnate.

We also need to learn to be able to tell the difference between what is just man's movement and what is genuinely the movement of the Holy Spirit. However, if we are unsure which is occurring, we must not shut down all movement in a church. Some people get afraid of man moving so they shut down all movement and in doing so shut down and quench the true and genuine move of the Holy Spirit. The solution is to learn to tell what is of Him and what is not. We need to teach people in the church to be mature with the move of the Holy Spirit rather than shutting it down out of fear. Remember, no matter how big or elaborate the box is that we use to constrain the Spirit of God, it will always be too small!

The Holy Spirit has ways of moving that we need to become sensitive to and learn to flow with. We need to learn how to flow with Him, to be sensitive to His flowing rather than trying to swim against the current and go upstream. You can go with Him or against Him. When we miss this, we miss the Holy Spirit altogether because we either quench or grieve Him.

Often what we do is we decide the direction we want to go and expect Him to follow us. We want the Holy Spirit to move in the direction we dictate, but that is not how it works. He is the river we must flow with. This takes spiritual sensitivity. It takes being able to recognize when and where He is flowing and then to respond to that.

In order to do that, people trying to flow with Him need to have a relationship with Him and have regular fellowship with Him. Spending regular and consistent time in God's presence through prayer and time in His Word prepares us to be more sensitive so we can flow with Him. Those who spend very little time in prayer or in the Word of God end up being more naturally minded and thus are less spiritually sensitive. Flowing with the Holy Spirit requires spiritual sensitivity which is only developed through an ongoing personal relationship with God.

I can attest to that personally as I was a very left brained kind of person and always needed to understand every little detail before I would commit to anything. That is not a good way to learn how the flow of the Spirit works. But, as I persisted in the Word and in prayer, the Holy Spirit helped me become more sensitive to Him and His leading. In fact, He has personally seen to my tutoring in the School of the Spirit for the last dozen years or more. And, I am much more sensitive to Him now than I was and am becoming more so all the time through the continuing presence and training by the Spirit of God. What an awesome adventure and privilege it is to be led and trained by the Holy Spirit!

Then, once we recognize the Spirit is flowing, we need to respond. Some people just want to sit and observe, or sit back and not participate. What that creates or sets up is an obstacle or impediment to His flow. When you put an obstacle in a rivers path, it blocks it and the river has to go around. Anything that is static in a rivers path, not moving or flowing with the river, is an obstacle to it. When enough obstacles are laid down, it totally blocks the flow of the river, causing a dam. When a dam is built, the flow stops.

People stand in the way of the flow of the Holy Spirit by not responding to Him. In some places, there are so many people not flowing and creating obstacles that the entire flow gets shut down. Some people who think they are being very spiritual by not responding to the Holy Spirit are actually blocking His movement. This is why He often has to go around them or gets stopped altogether. We see this in Jesus' own hometown:

Mark 6:4 But Jesus said unto them, A prophet is not without honour, but in his own country, and among his own kin, and in his own house. 5 And he could there do no mighty work, save that he laid his hands upon a few sick folk, and healed them. 6 And he marvelled because of their unbelief. And he went round about the villages, teaching.

Note that He could do no mighty works. In other words, He was prevented or blocked from doing them. This means the anointing of the Holy Spirit could not do what He wanted to do. Why? The people were blocking Him. This is because they knew Him and His family and were too familiar with Him. In essence, they were offended by His knowledge and His authority.

Some churches have learned to flow with the Spirit of God and welcome Him at every meeting. They will turn the meeting over to the Holy Spirit and allow Him to have full reign in their meetings and gatherings. This is as it should be. After all, He is sovereign. Remember, Jesus did all His works and miracles through the anointing of the Holy Spirit.

Acts 10:38 How God anointed Jesus of Nazareth with the Holy Spirit and with power: who went about doing good, and healing all that were oppressed of the devil; for God was with him.

Just like there are different rivers, with different strengths and flows, so there is diversity in the Holy Spirit. There can be different streams that come together and make up a river. The Holy Spirit has diversity. There is anointing for healing, intercession, joy, peace, praise, prayer and worship.

I am not talking about men calling a prayer meeting, or a time of praise and worship. I am talking about when God's people are united together and an anointing of prayer comes into the place, or an anointing for worship. At times like these, if people will respond, they can enter into a flow and move of the Spirit of God that will bring tremendous blessing.

What do I mean by respond? Well it is simple really. If a move of the Holy Spirit comes in to worship, and we all just sit there and look at each other, we are not responding! Not responding is not moving or flowing and is the same as a rock that stands in the path of a river that is trying to flow. We become an obstacle and the flow either has to go around it or is stopped by it. If an anointing to pray comes in and we just want to keep praising, we are going a different direction than the flow. There are times we get so into our programs and routines that the Holy Spirit is limited in what He can do. I am not saying we should not have an agenda, but we need to ensure we have the flexibility to allow Him to change it. After all, He is sovereign.

If the agenda says it is time to sing the last worship song, then have the announcements; and while we are singing an anointing to praise comes in, then we have a choice: go with the agenda or respond to Him. If there is an anointing to praise, then we should respond by joy, praise and shouting. Flowing with the anointing brings greater blessing than just sticking to our original program. We see the allowing the Spirit to flow, so little in churches, that what I am saying may be completely foreign to some people!

We need to be able to discern what the Spirit is doing and flow with that! Going a direction He is not going is like trying to paddle your boat upstream instead of flowing with the direction the river is going. The key is in being sensitive to what is right at any particular time. That takes time and patience to learn to understand His flow. We can learn to tell the difference between the move of the Holy Spirit of peace and that of joy. This takes developing sensitivity to His flow. It takes spending time with Him in prayer, and developing closeness of fellowship and relationship. We all respond to this at a different rate and intensity because of our unique passion and steadfastness in the things of the Lord.

The flow of the Holy Spirit comes out of our hearts, not our heads. It is not an intellectual thing. We need to give ourselves and others grace so we can all proceed and grow in the things of the Spirit, at the pace of the Holy Spirit as it is He who leads us and trains us in His ways. Spending time developing your relationship with God through prayer and the Word will increase your sensitivity to your heart. It is one thing to know that the Spirit is present and that the anointing is here, and it is another thing to know what the anointing is here for!

We must learn to interpret the flow, and sense the direction the Spirit is going and fall in line with Him. He is Lord and we can trust the Spirit to teach us His ways. We can ask the Spirit to help us and train us.

Dear heavenly Father, please help us to become more sensitive to the Holy Spirit's leading and to His flow. Please teach us your ways and the ways of the Spirit. Make our hearts teachable and sensitive to your Spirit Father. In Jesus' name we pray. Amen.

The River of Life

"Love is the river of life in the world." ~ Henry Ward Beecher

Whenever I think about the flow of the Holy Spirit I remember a river that flows from the throne of God. During the Feast of Tabernacles, the Jewish people took part in a water drawing ceremony on the last day of the feast. They would go down to the Pool of Siloam, draw water and bring it to the Temple Mount. Then they would pour out the water and recite Isaiah 12:2:

Isaiah 12:2 Behold, God is my salvation; I will trust, and not be afraid: for the LORD JEHOVAH is my strength and my song; he also is become my salvation. 3 Therefore with joy shall ye draw water out of the wells of salvation.

In Hebrew, the word salvation and Yeshua (Jesus, in Hebrew), are the same. When I hear about wells of salvation, my mind races to the last chapter in the bible, Revelation 22:

Revelation 22:1 And he shewed me a pure river of water of life, clear as crystal, proceeding out of the throne of God and of the Lamb. 2 In the midst of the street of it, and on either side of the river, was there the tree of life, which bare twelve manner of fruits, and yielded her fruit every month: and the leaves of the tree were for the healing of the nations.

Imagine the scene at the time of Jesus' appearance. In the middle of this ceremony, He stands up and shouts:

John 7:37 In the last day, that great day of the feast, Jesus stood and cried, saying, If any man thirst, let him come unto me, and drink. 38 He that believeth on me, as the scripture hath said, out of his belly shall flow rivers of living water.

Now, we have the wells of salvation, the river of life and rivers of living water flowing out of our belly. They are all tied together and represent the life giving and life sustaining power of God. There is

The River of Life

another river also discussed at length in the book of the prophet Ezekiel that parallels the verse quoted from Revelation 22:

Ezekiel 47:3 And when the man that had the line in his hand went forth eastward, he measured a thousand cubits, and he brought me through the waters; the waters were to the ankles. 4 Again he measured a thousand, and brought me through the waters; the waters were to the knees. Again he measured a thousand, and brought me through; the waters were to the loins. 5 Afterward he measured a thousand; and it was a river that I could not pass over: for the waters were risen, waters to swim in, a river that could not be passed over. 6 And he said unto me, Son of man, hast thou seen this? Then he brought me, and caused me to return to the brink of the river. 7 Now when I had returned, behold, at the bank of the river were very many trees on the one side and on the other. 8 Then said he unto me, These waters issue out toward the east country, and go down into the desert, and go into the sea: which being brought forth into the sea, the waters shall be healed. 9 And it shall come to pass, that everything that liveth, which moveth, whithersoever the rivers shall come, shall live: and there shall be a very great multitude of fish, because these waters shall come thither: for they shall be healed; and everything shall live whither the river cometh. ... 12 And by the river upon the bank thereof, on this side and on that side, shall grow all trees for meat, whose leaf shall not fade, neither shall the fruit thereof be consumed: it shall bring forth new fruit according to his months, because their waters they issued out of the sanctuary: and the fruit thereof shall be for meat, and the leaf thereof for medicine.

These promises are especially true for us today. Our Messiah is the same yesterday, today and forever. He did not promise a sprinkling or a tiny stream. He promised rivers of living water springing up within believers unto eternal life. Jesus gives life and refreshment to those who come to him and believe in him. Those who receive the gift of the Holy Spirit have a flowing well of refreshment and salvation within themselves, not just for their own benefit, but rivers of living water that flow out of their heart to give life, refreshment and salvation to others. In verse 9, the scripture talks about everything that comes to these waters will live. In my mind, I see the living water, the river of life that flows from us as life itself. We bring healing, light and life wherever we allow this flowing water to proceed from us.

Hebrews 13:8 Jesus Christ the same yesterday, and to day, and for ever.

Claim His promise today! Claim the fullness of life that is in Him! To draw life from Him, we must go to Him; one cannot draw water from a spring unless he goes to the spring. So, go to the spring that never runs dry, go to the spring of Yeshua (salvation)! Draw from Him the peace that surpasses all understanding. Draw from Him pure love, agape love. Draw from Him the joy that makes the trees clap. Draw all that you need; He is ready to let those waters flow abundantly to all who draw on them.

Isaiah 44:3 For I will pour water upon him that is thirsty, and floods upon the dry ground: I will pour my spirit upon thy seed, and my blessing upon thine offspring:

This river flows into us, and then through us to touch other people as we walk in faith, in love and in the anointing of the Holy Spirit. We need to continue to allow the Lord's living water to flow through us so we are constantly renewed, preserved and strengthened by its presence. This ever-renewing vitality of God's living water always flows through faith in the shed blood of Jesus!

Revelation 21:6 And he said unto me, It is done. I am Alpha and Omega, the beginning and the end. I will give unto him that is athirst of the fountain of the water of life freely.

Revelation 22:17 And the Spirit and the bride say, Come. And let him that heareth say, Come. And let him that is athirst come. And whosoever will, let him take the water of life freely.

The river of life, really living waters are God's power, compassion and love poured out on us, and poured out through us as we respond to the unction of the Holy Spirit. The power belongs to God, as He is the source, but we can be useful vessels, containers and conduits. This living water comes from God, but flows through his people to bring life and refreshment to others. Living waters are those that are moving, flowing and in constant motion. Many people think the only way to be baptized is with living or moving water such in as a stream, a creek or a river.

The notion of being a conduit, a pipe, or a hose that is used by God to disperse His awesome life and power is one analogy of the flowing of the Holy Spirit. If we are His, then we carry His light, His power (anointing) and His life everywhere we go. Thus, in a very real sense, every place we set our foot becomes kingdom territory as we claim it by our very presence. We are therefore light bearers and bearers of the living water of the river of life! How awesome is that?

Father, please make this truth real in our hearts and minds so we can be light and life wherever we go. Help us remember we are yours and that your life flows through us as we walk in your Spirit. Help us attain the fullness of your Spirit in Jesus' name. Amen.

Warrior Anointing

"I want the presence of God Himself, or I do not want anything at all to do with religion...I want all that God has or I do not want any." ~ A.W. Tozer

"Lead, follow, or get out of the way." ~ Thomas Paine.

Romans 8:14 For as many as are led by the Spirit of God, they are the sons of God.

Romans 8:19 For the earnest expectation of the creature waiteth for the manifestation of the sons of God.

Malachi 3:16-17 Then they that feared the LORD spake often one to another: and the LORD hearkened, and heard it, and a book of remembrance was written before him for them that feared the LORD, and that thought upon his name. 17 And they shall be mine, saith the LORD of hosts, in that day when I make up my jewels; and I will spare them, as a man spareth his own son that serveth him.

1 John 3:2 Beloved, now are we the sons of God, and it doth not yet appear what we shall be: but we know that, when he shall appear, we shall be like him; for we shall see him as he is.

Warrior Anointing

After defining what the anointing is and what it is all about, I wanted to answer the question, "what is the Warrior Anointing?" Then, we can focus on how to become anointed warriors which is what we are all called and destined to be.

The Warrior Anointing I am speaking and writing about is an anointing to change the world we live in. It is given to those who are completely sold out to God and who will obey God at all costs. We are not called to be timid or to be conformed to this world, but to change this world by our very presence. When we walk into a room, the atmosphere changes simply because we are there and we carry the true light within us.

1 John 2:10 He that loveth his brother abideth in the light, and there is none occasion of stumbling in him.

The central idea is that of warrior-hood. Every boy in a Native American village spent their nights dreaming of becoming a warrior someday. His days and indeed his whole life centered on that one idea. Thus, the notion of becoming a warrior consumed all the boys in the village and they devoted all of their time and effort to preparing for exactly that. No matter what occupation each boy may later take, he would always strive to become a fighting man, or warrior. Even tribes who did not live for war trained their young men to become fighting men. Their greatest profession in life was that of warrior-hood.

Every man would die, and many did, to attain the rank of a warrior. A boy who refused to become a warrior, and there were not many, was called woman-like, and was banned from the tribe. His life was in danger from his own clan members because he dishonored them. A man may not become anything more than just a warrior, but as long as a man tried to be a warrior, he was fully accepted by his people. Mothers would rather see their son brought home as a dead hero than as an alive coward.

Somewhere in my childhood, growing up in Northeastern Oklahoma's Cherokee County these same ideas and notions filled my little brain. I spent every spare second either in the forest hunting or on some body of water fishing. I truly loved it. I taught myself how to walk silently over dead leaves and dried twigs. I learned to read sign and tracked everything that moved in the woods until it became easy to read and I could follow anything that moved. I had an uncle, my Uncle Roy, who could hit a fox squirrel running up a tree in the eye with a .22 rifle at a hundred yards–every time. I learned how to shoot a rifle, a shotgun, a bow and arrow and could throw a pretty mean rock too. I learned how to still myself so game would walk right up to me.

I was in my element. I knew then this was what I was created for. I felt God's presence all around me and with me, every day. I did not really know Him, but I knew He was with me. I knew deep down inside that I was a warrior and destined for greatness.

There is another analogy from Native American tribes where a warrior may be known as a stake warrior. This term comes from the practice of staking oneself to the ground during battle. This prevents the warrior from retreating. A staked warrior is determined to fight until the end either through to victory or to give his life in the attempt. Staking himself to the ground also clearly tells his enemies his intentions. This reminds me of Shammah:

2 Samuel 23:11 And after him was Shammah the son of Agee the Hararite. And the Philistines were gathered together into a troop, where was a piece of ground full of lentils: and the people fled from the Philistines. 12 But he stood in the midst of the ground, and defended it, and slew the Philistines: and the LORD wrought a great victory.

If we are really warriors for Jesus, we should be as determined as a stake warrior to fight until we achieve victory, or go down in the attempt. For all that we hold dear, all that we love and cherish; we must be ready to give our all. What was learned in the natural now has to be brought into focus for character training.

This anointing, the warrior anointing, really is to take back what the enemy has stolen, to set the captives free, to present salvation to all, to deliver those that are oppressed and to heal the sick, the lame and the blind. It is a combination anointing of the priest, the prophet and the kingly anointing. Those who bear it will not be satisfied with the status quo but will always strive to improve the lot of those they encounter that are in bondage or deception.

What is a warrior lifestyle like? For my purposes in this book, I define warrior traits as: courage, discipline, faithfulness, generosity, honesty, honor, integrity, tenacity, truthfulness and wisdom. We are beacons of light, hope and truth. We are like the knights of old who do good everywhere we go. People can look to us for help no matter what is against them. We will do no wrong willfully. We will pray with fervor and tenacity and we will intercede for those who cannot intercede for themselves. We will share everything we have right down to the last crumb because we know our provision comes from Lord God Jehovah Jireh, our provider.

The true warrior is a very rare person indeed. Our choices are different and most people cannot understand why we live the way we do. We live life with a different set of values compared with the rest of society. Even those who share the same values, rarely live a lifestyle which adheres to those values to the same extent that a warrior does. For most people, ethics are situational. Most people make decisions according to what is best for them, instead of what is truly right. This is not the case with a warrior. The warrior values honor, integrity, justice, and a sense of what is right, above all else. Therefore, for a warrior ethics are not situational; they are his way of life.

John 8:23 And he said unto them, Ye are from beneath; I am from above: ye are of this world; I am not of this world.

The warrior lifestyle includes a code of ethics which is non-negotiable. The warrior's code of ethics, or code of honor, is taken very seriously. To a warrior, distinguishing between right and wrong is of the utmost importance. He sees right and wrong in terms of black and white. It is all about good versus evil. He knows that every action is either honorable or dishonorable. There is no gray area for a warrior as grey is just a lighter shade of black.

If we are In Christ, in the beloved, then these scriptures are for us:

2 Corinthians 1:19 For the Son of God, Jesus Christ, who was preached among you by us, *even* by me and Silvanus and Timotheus, was not yea and nay, but in him was yea. 20 For all the promises of God in him *are* yea, and in him Amen, unto the glory of God by us. 21 Now he which stablisheth us with you in Christ, and hath anointed us, *is* God;

1 John 2:27 But the anointing which ye have received of him abideth in you, and ye need not that any man teach you: but as the same anointing teacheth you of all things, and is truth, and is no lie, and even as it hath taught you, ye shall abide in him.

We are anointed by God. God says so and we need to just receive that and believe it. As we discussed earlier, in the Old Testament, anointing was reserved for only three special servants of God: for kings, priests and prophets. King David, and Jesus were anointed in all three of these offices. And, we are also anointed in all three aspects if we will dedicate ourselves to try and live holy lives before God.

Jesus was anointed as a priest, even as our high priest. Now, since we are redeemed by Jesus we are not only anointed, but we are anointed as priests of God:

1 Peter 2:5 Ye also, as lively stones, are built up a spiritual house, an holy priesthood, to offer up spiritual sacrifices, acceptable to God by Jesus Christ.

1 Peter 2:9 But ye *are* a chosen generation, a royal priesthood, an holy nation, a peculiar people; that ye should shew forth the praises of him who hath called you out of darkness into his marvellous light:

It gets even better because we are also anointed as kings:

Revelation 20:6 Blessed and holy *is* he that hath part in the first resurrection: on such the second death hath no power, but they shall be priests of God and of Christ, and shall reign with him a thousand years.

Revelation 1:5 And from Jesus Christ, *who is* the faithful witness, *and* the first begotten of the dead, and the prince of the kings of the earth. Unto him that loved us, and washed us from our sins in his own blood, 6 And hath made us kings and priests unto God and his Father; to him *be* glory and dominion for ever and ever. Amen.

Revelation 5:10 And hast made us unto our God kings and priests: and we shall reign on the earth.

Jesus Himself has made us kings and priests! So, we will not only serve God and men, but we will reign as kings on the earth. King David was a warrior king who was anointed as king, priest and prophet. Finally, we are also anointed as prophets:

Acts 2:17 And it shall come to pass in the last days, saith God, I will pour out of my Spirit upon all flesh: and your sons and your daughters shall prophesy, and your young men shall see visions, and your old men shall dream dreams:

1 Corinthians 14:31 For ye may all prophesy one by one, that all may learn, and all may be comforted.

I had asked the Lord what He wanted to call this effort. A few days later I heard "The Warrior Anointing" in my spirit on my way to the county jail to conduct an Experiencing God class. This was in September of 2011. I started researching it the next day and with the leading of the Holy Spirit discovered it is not something to seek, but rather something to receive and then to pass on to others as they fully commit to the warrior lifestyle...

The anointing of the Holy Spirit that we receive when we are fully committed to serve Jesus is the anointing of a king, a priest, and a prophet. When one was chosen to be a priest, he was anointed with oil symbolic of the Holy Spirit coming upon him and giving him power, wisdom and ability for the task set before him. The same was true when a king was anointed and again when a prophet was anointed. This leads me to some conclusions.

1. The anointing comes when accepting a new responsibility. When a warrior accepts a new responsibility, he will be anointed by the Holy Spirit for that task. Any new task for which a child of God is chosen and any new responsibility that God gives him is important enough that the Holy Spirit will anoint him for this new responsibility.

2. This anointing equips one for a task. Whom God calls, He qualifies, He equips and He prepares. When a warrior is called to a new responsibility, he needs to be equipped. Therefore, he needs to be anointed by the Holy Spirit as God provides him what he needs to fulfill this new calling.

3. The warrior simply yields to the Spirit for this anointing. We do not need to struggle, or beg and plead for something that God freely gives us.

4. God gives His approval and His support to the endeavor by giving us His anointing.

1 John 2:27 But the anointing which ye have received of him abideth in you, and ye need not that any man teach you: but as the same anointing teacheth you of all things, and is truth, and is no lie, and even as it hath taught you, ye shall abide in him.

1 Corinthians 16:13 Watch ye, stand fast in the faith, quit you like men, be strong.

The warrior anointing is to open doors, and to lead the way to show people they can be more than they thought they could be. It gives people permission to dream large and to experience God for themselves in ways unheard of in traditional denominational churches.

Further, it presents a manner of fellowship, encouragement, development and opportunity to equip and prepare people for a powerful life of destiny. It releases people to find their inheritance, to live and walk in the favor of the Most High, to live and give out of abundance and blessing in such a way that it will transform their families, churches and communities.

Did you know that God never stopped asking people to build arks? He is still calling on men and women today to have a long-term goal for their lives. Most call it their destiny, something that can only be entered into through a vision that comes directly from God. And, these goals are something that they and only they, have been asked to do. But be sure of this, whenever a vision from God is conceived in our hearts, the enemy will do everything he possibly can to either take us off course or kill the vision before it ever gets off the ground.

Hebrews 12:14 Follow peace with all men, and holiness, without which no man shall see the Lord:

There is only one way that the arks of our lives can be built; by choosing to be holy, one day at a time. Holiness is not the dreadful legalism of religious bigotry, but is simply doing today what God requires of us to do today; and, being clean and pure from the ravages of sin! Holiness is being like God who is holy. John summed it up in an amazingly simple way by saying "walk as Jesus did!"

1 John 2:6 He that saith he abideth in him ought himself also so to walk, even as he walked.

So what did Jesus do? Jesus only went where the Father told Him to go. He only did what the Father told Him to do. He only said what the Father told Him to say. The conclusion of His life of daily obedience was not the building of a physical ark that saved one family, but the opening of the gates of salvation to all who will believe and receive Him – for He is the only way of salvation.

John 14:6 Jesus saith unto him, I am the way, the truth, and the life: no man cometh unto the Father, but by me.

We are being called to rise to a new level, and receive a new anointing to walk as spiritual warriors. We need to get alone with God. Ask Him to equip us and anoint us to walk in this new calling. When you are ready to dedicate yourself to walk in this new level, pray this prayer for the impartation of the Warrior Anointing (also listed in Appendix C) and receive this anointing by praying with all your heart the prayer listed there. Trust God to make it so in your life, and He will.

Dear heavenly Father, in the name of Jesus I ask you to come precious Holy Spirit and settle on me right now. Rest on me in all your fullness and glory. In the name of Jesus, I ask for and receive the impartation of the Warrior Anointing of God Most High.

This anointing is a breaker anointing that will empower me to live above the snake line and to walk in dunamis power as I walk in the Spirit. This anointing will cause the enemy and his forces to flee from the mighty power of God that rests on me. The enemy's forces cannot stand against me as I walk in divine favor in every aspect of my life. I walk in divine protection and am guarded at all times by mighty warring angels.

I am empowered with great faith, great peace, great love, a sound mind, a kind and gentle spirit, great self-control, great generosity and great wisdom in all matters pertaining to the advancement of the kingdom of God. I walk in the favor of the Most High.

Father, bless me now with your presence, your glory and your power to do all You created me to do in the matchless name of Jesus, the Anointed One!

Amen and Amen

This anointing, the Warrior Anointing is something we are to receive and walk in NOW. This is the anointing we need NOW so we can learn to walk holy before God and man and bring in the last great harvest, the last great revival.

The rest of this book discusses how that is done, how to walk as a warrior and stand against all the things this world and our enemy will throw at us. But, remember we do this from a position of victory.

If you prayed to receive this anointing, you have chosen wisely and have begun heading down the road on the greatest adventure of your life! Walk in the Warrior Anointing and never doubt for one minute that this is God's will for you and for your life. He wants us to succeed and finish the work Jesus began:

1 John 3:8 ... For this purpose the Son of God was manifested, that he might destroy the works of the devil.

Father, we love you with all our heart and soul, all our mind and all our might. We pray for wisdom, knowledge and understanding of you, Jesus, the Holy Spirit, your Word and your anointing. Teach us your ways and help us all to walk in your light and in your ways full of your Holy Spirit, being led of your Spirit every moment of our lives this day.

Father, please help us to be light to everyone we encounter and to bring other people to a greater awareness and knowledge of you and your ways in everything we do and say. Help us walk in love and declare your awesome holiness and love with every act of our lives and every word that crosses our lips. Help us bring glory to you and to Jesus with our lives and help us exalt you with every breath we take. In the mighty name of Jesus, the Anointed One we pray. Amen.

Prepare for Battle

"One of these days some simple soul will pick up the book of God, read it, and believe it. Then the rest of us will be embarrassed." ~Leonard Ravenhill

Isaiah 66:2 For all those *things* hath mine hand made, and all those *things* have been, saith the LORD: but to this *man* will I look, *even* to *him that is* poor and of a contrite spirit, and trembleth at my word.

Leviticus 19:2 Speak unto all the congregation of the children of Israel, and say unto them, Ye shall be holy: for I the LORD your God *am* holy.

"At the timberline where the storms strike with the most fury, the sturdiest trees are found." ~ Hudson Taylor.

We have an ancient, relentless and ruthless enemy whose sole aim is to kill, steal and destroy the inheritance and destiny of the people who call Jesus their Lord and Master. If we claim we belong to Jesus, then satan and all of his hoards and minions are going to attack us and our families. We have a choice. We can bury our heads in the sand and pretend he is not there and hope he will go away and leave us alone. Of course, he will not. Or, we can prepare ourselves to face him and his forces and to stand our ground refusing to be led or pulled off course.

There is a method in his madness. He knows he does not need another spirit-filled Christian who knows who he is in Christ and what he is capable of, running amuck in his kingdom. So, he directs many of his forces to prevent us from learning who we are in Christ Jesus. Then, if we do learn who we are, his attack will change focus to what we can accomplish. If he can convince us that we are nothing but "a poor sinner saved by grace" with no real power or authority, and certainly no power to stand against his wiles, he wins.

This battle rages in our minds. Every sin begins as a thought and as we give it a place in us by dwelling on it, fantasizing about it and mulling it over and over; it will become an act against Almighty God known as sin. That is just the way it is. There is no getting around this. When we sin, we sin against God. We have to face it and deal with it, head to head. Every sin begins in our minds.

Therefore, preparing for battle primarily means preparing our minds to accept and dwell on the truth, and on good things rather than dark things. Spiritual warfare is an offensive battle tactic. We resist the devil before his minions begin their assault and again when his hoards harass us. We develop and adhere to spiritual disciplines that make us stronger and better prepared to face the enemy. We seek out and engage the enemy when we see people in spiritual bondage. We use prayer as a weapon to penetrate strongholds that cannot be reached in any other way. Spiritual warfare puts aside passive attitudes which keep us on the bench and out of the game. Instead of seeking our own agendas, we submit and surrender to God and accept the sacrifices He calls us to make.

We need a strategy if we are going to be successful in our fight against the evil, lust and wiles of this world. The first thing we need to do is prepare ourselves as best we can for the battles ahead. Just accept the fact that battles are coming and some of them will be ferocious. The better we prepare ourselves the better we can withstand them. In this reference, I propose to teach others how to learn to stand. This is mostly a question of character.

In order to begin, we need a clear understanding of who our enemy is, and who God is to us. We need to understand who we are in Christ and what power we possess based on Jesus' own words. We need to learn how to die to the things that tempt us, and we need to learn how to access the power we hold within us. The remainder of this section will discuss those very topics and offer suggestions on how to implement the changes needed to become true spiritual warriors.

Dear heavenly Father, how glorious and wondrous you are! Please teach us how to prepare ourselves for the amazing days ahead. Please give us great courage and great strength to face the giants we must face and when we have done all we know to do, to stand trusting in you. You Lord are our high tower, our sanctuary and our refuge. Help us become all you created us to be in Jesus name. Amen.

Who is Our Enemy?

"Still fight resolutely on, knowing that, in this spiritual combat, none is overcome but he who ceases to struggle and to trust in God." ~ Lorenzo Scupoli

So, you are a new Christian huh? Get ready - whether you know it or not, the fight is on. You are marked by God and the enemy of your soul can see that, and he has declared war on you as his enemy and he will do everything in his power to kill you and those you love, to steal your inheritance and to destroy any good works you are supposed to accomplish. This enemy is completely merciless and vicious. He hates us as much as God loves us – simply because God does love us. There is no give in this ancient enemy and he is absolutely relentless and ruthless in his desire to destroy us, our lives and our loved ones. His name is satan. He is the accuser of the brethren. He stands before God accusing us day and night.

Revelation 12:10 And I heard a loud voice saying in heaven, Now is come salvation, and strength, and the kingdom of our God, and the power of his Christ: for the accuser of our brethren is cast down, which accused them before our God day and night.

What we must do is to prepare ourselves to wage war against a deadly and ferocious foe who has no morals, no qualms and no reservations about doing anything he can to take us down, or out of the picture altogether. This enemy will attack our finances, our minds, our homes, our children, our work situation and environment, our vehicles while we are driving, our dreams while we are sleeping, our integrity and our bodies, souls and spirits at every opportunity.

In Ezekiel we learn about this ancient adversary where he is described as the covering cherub who was perfect in beauty:

Ezekiel 28:12 Son of man, take up a lamentation upon the king of

Tyrus, and say unto him, Thus saith the Lord GOD; Thou sealest up the sum, full of wisdom, and perfect in beauty. 13 Thou hast been in Eden the garden of God; every precious stone was thy covering, the sardius, topaz, and the diamond, the beryl, the onyx, and the jasper, the sapphire, the emerald, and the carbuncle, and gold: the workmanship of thy tabrets and of thy pipes was prepared in thee in the day that thou wast created. 14 Thou art the anointed cherub that covereth; and I have set thee so: thou wast upon the holy mountain of God; thou hast walked up and down in the midst of the stones of fire. 15 Thou wast perfect in thy ways from the day that thou wast created, till iniquity was found in thee.

And, again in Isaiah we learn more and why he fell from heaven after he thought he could take God's place.

Isaiah 14:12 How art thou fallen from heaven, O Lucifer, son of the morning! how art thou cut down to the ground, which didst weaken the nations! 13 For thou hast said in thine heart, I will ascend into heaven, I will exalt my throne above the stars of God: I will sit also upon the mount of the congregation, in the sides of the north: 14 I will ascend above the heights of the clouds; I will be like the most High. 15 Yet thou shalt be brought down to hell, to the sides of the pit.

Now, understand he is a completely vanquished and defeated foe. Jesus descended into hell and took the keys to hell and the grave away from him.

Revelation 1:18 I am he that liveth, and was dead; and, behold, I am alive for evermore, Amen; and have the keys of hell and of death.

Lord, please give us insight and wisdom about our position in Christ and how to stand against the enemy of our souls. Help us to see past the wiles and temptations we face and see the real culprit so we can stand strong. Give us supernatural understanding of the ferocity of the battle raging in the heavens. In the name of Jesus we pray. Amen.

What Does the Enemy Look Like?

"The chief danger of the church today is that it is trying to get on the same side as the world, instead of turning the world upside down. Our Master expects us to accomplish results, even if they bring opposition and conflict. Anything is better than compromise, apathy, and paralysis. God give to us an intense cry for the old-time power of the Gospel of the Holy Ghost!" ~ A.B Simpson

Proverbs 26:2 As the bird by wandering, as the swallow by flying, so the curse causeless shall not come.

Identifying the enemy - just as there are heavenly beings, there are also satanic beings. To be spiritually prepared for battle, we must determine who the real enemy is. Our preparation for spiritual warfare requires application of the spiritual principles revealed to us in the Word of God.

Just what is spiritual warfare? Spiritual warfare for the Christian is about truth versus lies, love versus hatred, good versus evil, and the integrity of God's Word. These aspects are experienced in the physical realms of the world, in our flesh and especially in our minds. Our weapons of warfare are found in the wisdom of Christ: God's Word and the Holy Spirit.

Our enemy is not flesh and blood that we can strike him down with a blow or with a sword. He is an ancient enemy who once led the worship of God in heaven itself. We must never underestimate the capabilities of our adversary or the deceptiveness he will use in his attempt to defeat us in spiritual battle.

satan does not fight alone. Up until today, there are spirits over every country that rule that country and over every city that rule that city. These are the forces referred to by the Apostle Paul when he wrote:

Ephesians 6:12 For we wrestle not against flesh and blood, but against principalities, against powers, against the rulers of the darkness of this world, against spiritual wickedness in high places.

These are the five divisions of satan's forces:

1. Spirits or demons. "We wrestle not against flesh and blood."

2. Principalities - forces and dominions dealing with nations and governments; high-level satanic princes set over nations and regions of the earth; commanding generals over satan's fallen army. The concept of principalities is understood by the Greek word arche meaning chief or ruler. These principalities are ruling devil spirits possessing executive authority or governmental rule in the world. These ruling entities usually involve a particular nation, people or race.

3. Powers - having authority and power of action in spheres open to them; supernatural and natural government; high ranking powers of evil. The Greek word for "powers" is exousia which means derived or conferred authority, the warrant or right to do something, or delegated influences of control.

4. Rulers of darkness of this world - governing the darkness and blindness of the world at large; operate within countries and cultures to influence certain aspects of life; governing spirits of darkness.

5. Spiritual wickedness In high places - forces being directed in and upon the Church of Jesus Christ in wiles, fiery darts, onslaughts and every conceivable deception about doctrine which they are capable of planning; the many types of evil spirits that commonly afflict people; the collective body of demon soldiers comprising Satan's hordes. The Greek word for wickedness is ponēria and means depravity and particularly in the sense of malice and mischief, plots, sins, and iniquity.

Ephesians 2:2 Wherein in time past ye walked according to the course of this world, according to the prince of the power of the air, the spirit that now worketh in the children of disobedience:

What Does the Enemy Look Like

Since satan is the prince of the power of the air, these wicked spirits, in high places, are often understood to be the collective organization of all of satan's devil spirits. These malevolent spirits work evil and mischief and operate in our atmosphere. All kinds of spiritual filth are propagated, in these realms, for the purpose of humanity's deception and subsequent destruction. Before we became a Christian we too walked according to the prince of the power of the air.

How do we engage in spiritual warfare against demons, principalities, powers, rulers of the darkness of this world, and spiritual wickedness? We need to be strong in the Lord to fight the battles we face to become valiant men of God and fulfill our destinies. We prepare for battle and deliverance, not only by identifying the enemy, but also by coming to terms with who we are in Christ, clarifying our resolve and girding up our strength. It is vital to understand that the strength we need to defeat and subdue the enemy of our souls is not found in the natural – in our flesh; it is only found in the Lord and in His ways. The Bible commands us as believers to:

Ephesians 6:10 Finally, my brethren, be strong in the Lord, and in the power of his might.

Strength in the Lord is obtained as we recognize who we are in Christ and acknowledge that He is the real source of our strength. We should not attempt to fight the demonic forces of hell alone, for the power to defeat and subdue the enemy does not rest in our strength; it always comes from the Lord:

Luke 10:19 Behold, I give unto you power to tread on serpents and scorpions, and over all the power of the enemy: and nothing shall by any means hurt you.

If we are strong in the Lord, the enemy will attack the weakest member of our family in his attempts to get us to stop talking about Jesus and obeying God. If we compromise with sin in any way, we open a door to him and his forces to openly come in and attack us, to set up camp and stay, and in general to become a fixture in and around our lives. He and his forces continually watch us and assess our strengths and weaknesses so they can come against us. They will not attack us in our strength but always where we are weakest and most vulnerable.

As I said, when we sin we open a door to the enemy and his forces they can use to attack us or those we love. When we confess that sin to God and repent, God closes that door. Our enemy is vicious, but he only has power over us where we let him have power over us. He was soundly defeated at Calvary where he lost the keys to death and hell to our precious Lord Jesus, the Anointed One. He is a completely defeated foe, but as long as we refuse to rise up and take the authority Jesus gave us, satan can and will attack us and those we cherish. We must stand against him and all his wicked wiles.

Revelation 1:18 I am he that liveth, and was dead; and, behold, I am alive for evermore, Amen; and have the keys of hell and of death.

We have to do this for ourselves, our families and our communities. When Jesus left this world to return to His Father, he gave us His authority and told us to use it:

Matthew 28:18 And Jesus came and spoke unto them, saying, All power is given unto me in heaven and in earth. 19 Go you therefore, and teach all nations, baptizing them in the name of the Father, and of the Son, and of the Holy Spirit: 20 Teaching them to observe all things whatsoever I have commanded you: and, lo, I am with you always, even unto the end of the world. Amen.

If we do not rise up and take back that which is rightfully ours, who will? If we do not rise up and defend our families, who will? Those poor souls who do not know Jesus or have Jesus as their Lord may be taken at will:

2 Timothy 2:26 And *that* they may recover themselves out of the

snare of the devil, who are taken captive by him at his will.

Oh Father, please give us wisdom and understanding about how easily we are deceived and led into areas where we become vulnerable. Please teach us how to discern the enemy and all of his tactics so we can stand against him in faith. In the name of Jesus we pray. Amen.

Snares of the Enemy

"If the child of God has come to appreciate the wiles of his assailant, he will not surrender at any point but will instead resist; and his emotional soul is thereby protected. Resistance in the inner man forces the enemy to go on the defensive." Watchman Nee

Proverbs 22:5 Thorns and snares are in the way of the froward: he that doth keep his soul shall be far from them.

Job 18:8 For he is cast into a net by his own feet, and he walketh upon a snare.

The enemy has laid out very careful, and well thought out snares to entrap men and he is very, very practical in his approach:

1. Kill would-be saints before they are born into this world through abortion or miscarriage.

2. If they survive this, then break up their homes through parental addiction, pornography, greed, pride or lust.

3. If they make it through this, they have to run the gauntlet of public schools where God, satan and hell are denied and morality is ridiculed. This continues from the time they are five years old until they are eighteen for high school students or twenty-two or later if college bound.

4. Beginning as early as possible, ensure they are constantly exposed to illicit sex, drugs and alcohol, violence and other vile and wicked devices designed to deceive them.

5. If they go to college, morality is non-existent and God is actively attacked and denigrated and they are told they can have anything they want – after all, they deserve it.

6. Continually bombard them through the air waves (he is the prince of the power of the air) with images of lust, greed, get rich quick schemes, violence and the fact that they should have all the luxuries they want – because after all, they deserve it.

7. Once they get a job, keep up the peer pressure at work, for bigger and better things to occupy their time and consume their resources. Always keep them focused on things that will satisfy the emptiness they feel; well – almost.

8. If someone were really talented (anointed), make them so prosperous or successful that all they think about is their money or their success, leaving no time for the Lord.

9. If one should escape from all this, get them into a church where they must be part of a group or clique and keep them as busy as possible with events and fund raisers and other activities – anything but preaching the pure Word of God or reaching out to the lost.

10. Ensure they pick up a religious mindset (evil spirit) whereby they are taught and feel that no church but theirs is righteous and therefore no church but theirs is assured salvation.

11. Ensure there are many rules they must strictly adhere to in order to be accepted in their church.

12. Create division in their church so church splits are easier to accommodate and make sure that truly righteous and on-fire Christians are never made to feel at home in their church because they are just too radical. If at all possible, re-create an atmosphere where Pharisees are easier to grow

and thrive.

13. Create an environment where the leaders of the church are isolated and the congregation can more easily murmur and criticize their actions, their sermons and their families.

14. Attack people with sickness and disease so that they can never be truly free to serve the Lord in any real capacity as they are continually assailed by one ailment after another.

15. As people age, afflict them with dementia, memory loss and foggy thinking so no one will listen or revere their words or their experiences.

You must make no mistake about it. This is a battle to the death. We will never be completely beyond the reach of our enemy until we are completely dead to sin, evil and temptation. Once we get "above the snake line," then he will go after our children, then our grandchildren. We must contend for our families as long as we draw breath!

The enemy has continued throughout history to attack the unborn, the newly born and the innocent. There are a number of things we can do to level the playing field, and even swing it over to our advantage, but we must be aware at all times that our enemy never sleeps and will never relent. He will do everything in his power to steal our inheritance and our destiny. satan is a liar and the father of it:

John 8:44 Ye are of *your* father the devil, and the lusts of your father ye will do. He was a murderer from the beginning, and abode not in the truth, because there is no truth in him. When he speaketh a lie, he speaketh of his own: for he is a liar, and the father of it.

Here are some of his favorite lies to us:

- We can live independent of God and be our own God
- God's Word is not trustworthy or authoritative

- We can disobey God's Word and get away with it
- We can define ourselves rather than letting God define us
- God is not good, and He does not want what is best for us
- We are not any good and will never amount to much
- Nobody, including God can tell us what to do; it is my life and I can make my own decisions
- We should follow our own desires, so life will turn out great for us
- We should go along with what other people are doing
- We are too weak to overcome sin, evil and temptation
- It is just a little sin, God really will not mind

The Father will never tell us to do things or speak to us in this manner for they are all traps from the enemy. He will never tell us to go places where we can satisfy the lusts of the flesh. He will never tell us to say things which put others down so that we can lift ourselves up. The Lord told us our weapons are mighty:

2 Corinthians 10:3 For though we walk in the flesh, we do not war after the flesh: 4 (For the weapons of our warfare *are* not carnal, but mighty through God to the pulling down of strong holds;) 5 Casting down imaginations, and every high thing that exalteth itself against the knowledge of God, and bringing into captivity every thought to the obedience of Christ; 6 And having in a readiness to revenge all disobedience, when your obedience is fulfilled.

What we need to do next is understand who God is to us, and who we are in Him.

Dear heavenly Father, help us to become aware of our enemy and his tactics against us. Please teach our hands to war against him using the tools and weapons you provide. Please help us to never fear him or his hoards or minions, but to always stand against him and all his wiles. Protect our families from all his plans and designs with a mighty wall of fire in Jesus name. Amen.

Who is God to You?

"God does not want us to know that He is faithful just because the Bible says so, but He wants to show Himself faithful in our lives."
~ Robert Ekh

We have to figure out for ourselves who God is to us. Is he a tough, mean old God who only answers prayers begrudgingly? Is he a small diminutive god (note the lowercase g) who is merely being amused and entertained by our suffering? Is he a vindictive and vengeful God who is looking for someone to punish or torment? Is your God aloof and distant?

For many of us, our image and conception of God probably stems from our relationship with our own natural fathers. If your dad was hard and harsh, you probably perceive God in that way too. If your dad was nonexistent, or at least not available to you for any reason, that would frame your reference to God. It could be he was really busy trying to make a living, or he made some mistakes in life and was incarcerated, or maybe he was consumed by some addiction. Whatever the case may be, if he was not available as much as you thought he should be or wished he could be, then your perception of God will be influenced by that.

Perhaps you had a great dad who loved you unconditionally and was available to you most of the time when you needed him and his influence in your life. But, perhaps something along the way during your life soured your relationship with one another in some way or another. Or, you just grew apart because your interests diverged from one another.

No matter what kind of relationship each of us had with our natural fathers, we need to come to terms with who God is to us right now. Jesus called God, Abba. Abba means daddy in Aramaic and is a term of endearment, of love. God is love:

1 John 4:8 He that loveth not knoweth not God; for God is love.

God has always existed just as He is and He does not change because He is not learning and growing like we are:

Malachi 3:6 For I *am* the LORD, I change not;

God is the same yesterday, today and tomorrow and does not change because He is already perfect and complete:

Hebrews 13:8 Jesus Christ the same yesterday, and to day, and for ever.

God is altogether good. He is good every single day. He does not get up in a bad mood. He is not dismayed by the events that are occurring in the world today. His arm is not any shorter than it ever was and His strength is not diminished in any aspect. God is altogether good. The Word of God describes Him: God is full of compassion (Psalm 78:38 and 111:4). He is long-suffering and plenteous in mercy and truth (Psalm 86:15). The Lord is gracious and full of compassion; slow to anger, and of great mercy. The Lord is good to all: and His tender mercies are all over His works (Psalm 145:8-9).

There is no badness or evil in God at all. He is all the good there is. He is 100 percent good, all the time. He is absolute goodness. In fact, God is so good that badness or evil cannot even exist in His presence. He is as good as good can be! He is so good that evil and badness will be consumed by His glory. That is why He had to hide Moses as His goodness passed before Moses. Otherwise, Moses would have been consumed by the glory of God's goodness because Moses was just a man and had sinned and was therefore contaminated by sin. But, God protected Moses and His goodness made a way for Moses to see the hinder parts of God.

God is an absolute marvel. He is more wonderful, more loving, more kind, more generous, more faithful and more awesome than any mind of man can imagine! My theology of God continues to evolve and change as I get to know Him better. My perception of God is not the same as it was when I was first saved, nor is it the same as it was even ten years ago. Every box I build to place God in, is too small and I think God gets a kick out of showing us how awesome and wondrous He really is.

If your perception of God is anything less than He is the most marvelous, wondrous and amazing God we could ever imagine, then your God is too small. I assert right now that with all our minds put together, we cannot really fathom how big, how wonderful and how loving our loving heavenly Father really is. We will have an eternity to get to know Him better and from what I have seen so far, it will take that long to come to a full understanding of Him, if we ever do!

So, if your God is too small, think deeply about these things before you go any further in this book:

The magnitude of God's love is absolutely staggering. It is not an on again, off again kind of love like human beings offer one another. 1 John 4:8 tells us "God is love." Since God is infinite, His capacity for love and to love is also infinite. He taught me how to love after I received Jesus. I thought I knew what love was but I really did not until He showed me. He is love and love is Him.

John 15:13 Greater love hath no man than this, that a man lay down his life for his friends.

1 John 3:16 Hereby perceive we the love *of God*, because he laid down his life for us: and we ought to lay down *our* lives for the brethren.

Since God is full of compassion (Psalm 78:38), it takes an infinite amount of compassion to fill Him up. Wow! That means that since it takes all the compassion there is to fill God up, then compassion is not a feeling or a thing – it is God! It is Him and He is compassion.

Psalms 78:38 But he, *being* full of compassion, forgave *their* iniquity, and destroyed *them* not: yea, many a time turned he his anger away, and did not stir up all his wrath.

Psalms 111:4 He hath made his wonderful works to be remembered: the LORD *is* gracious and full of compassion.

Once we come to grips with God's love and compassion, then we can proceed to learn His ways more fully.

Oh Father, please give us a deep revelation of how wonderful and good you really are. Help us to see and understand how awesome and magnificent you are in every aspect. Give us a greater expectation of miracles and wonders in our lives and in the lives of those we minister to. Give us holy boldness to declare your majesty, your might and your love to this lost and dying world we live in, in the matchless name of Jesus I pray. Amen.

Who Am I to God?

"The Son of God became a man to enable men to become sons of God." ~ C.S. Lewis

Psalms 139:23-24 Search me, O God, and know my heart: try me, and know my thoughts: 24 And see if there be any wicked way in me, and lead me in the way everlasting.

God has two powerful elements constantly at work in and on His chosen vessels. These are the Word of God and the Blood of the Lamb. We are constantly being washed by the application of the Word. And, we are justified and declared righteous through the Blood of the Lamb.

God does not look at us with disdain or loathing. He sees us as we will be when we are perfect as we will be in heaven. God calls things that are not as they will be and thus creates them to be what he desires them to be. Therefore, in His eyes we are already completed formed, glorified, perfected and we look like Jesus. When God looks at us, He sees Jesus.

Romans 4:17 ... calleth those things which be not as though they were.

When God smells us, He smells Jesus too. We are covered with the blood of the Lamb and when we enter God's presence, we are a sweet fragrance to Him. This is true because we are covered with the blood of the Lamb.

You see we are all in the process of becoming what God intended for us to be. Even though we cannot see it yet, we are in His grip and He will have His way in us. Our sanctification is a process that will produce men who look like Jesus.

2 Corinthians 3:18 But we all, with open face beholding as in a glass the glory of the Lord, are changed into the same image from glory to glory, even as by the Spirit of the Lord.

2 Timothy 2:21 If a man therefore purge himself from these, he shall be a vessel unto honour, sanctified, and meet for the master's use, and prepared unto every good work.

The Lord is cleaning us up. I tell people all the time not to try and get cleaned up before they come to Jesus. We come to Him just as we are, and He will clean us up. He will purge us of those things that do not belong, then prune and trim all the areas that need reshaping to fit who we are.

John 1:12 But as many as received him, to them gave he power to become the sons of God, even to them that believe on his name:

Yes! We are sons of God! The Lord tells us that we are His sons, and that we are in the process of becoming His sons. When we received Jesus, we became full-fledged members of the family of God. How awesome is that? As we learn to be led by the Spirit of God, this will take on greater meaning.

Romans 8:14 For as many as are led by the Spirit of God, they are the sons of God.

God tells us in His word that all of creation eagerly awaits the full manifestation of the sons of God, and that all of creation groans and struggles during the long wait for this to occur.

Romans 8:19 For the earnest expectation of the creature waiteth for the manifestation of the sons of God.

Romans 8:22 For we know that the whole creation groaneth and travaileth in pain together until now.

When we break through all the sin, the lies and the deception of the enemy and really come to terms with who we are in Christ Jesus, we will be blameless; even faultless. We will shine as beacons of light, of hope and honor. We will become pure vessels fit for service.

Philippians 2:15 That ye may be blameless and harmless, the sons of God, without rebuke, in the midst of a crooked and perverse nation, among whom ye shine as lights in the world;

Before we were born again, God knew we would one day choose Jesus as our Lord and Master. God is patient and He works in our lives at a pace that will not burn us out or burn us up.

1 John 3:1-3 Behold, what manner of love the Father hath bestowed upon us, that we should be called the sons of God: therefore the world knoweth us not, because it knew him not. 2 Beloved, now are we the sons of God, and it doth not yet appear what we shall be: but we know that, when he shall appear, we shall be like him; for we shall see him as he is. 3 And every man that hath this hope in him purifieth himself, even as he is pure.

We need to believe that we are indeed sons of God. We need to believe His Word and what it says about us! When you get up tomorrow and every day after that, pray:

Thank you Father for making me into one of your sons! Thank you Father that I am a true son of God. Help me to walk and live my life before you this day with that truth planted deep in my spirit. In Jesus' name I pray. Amen

Dunamis Power

"Trying to do the Lord's work in your own strength is the most confusing, exhausting, and tedious of all work. But when you are filled with the Holy Spirit, then the ministry of Jesus just flows out of you." ~ Corrie Ten Boom.

Isaiah 28:11 For with stammering lips and another tongue will he speak to this people.

Jesus imputed His authority to His disciples after His death and resurrection in two steps. First, he gave us a commission:

Matthew 28:18 And Jesus came and spake unto them, saying, All power is given unto me in heaven and in earth. 19 Go ye therefore, and teach all nations, baptizing them in the name of the Father, and of the Son, and of the Holy Ghost: 20 Teaching them to observe all things whatsoever I have commanded you: and, lo, I am with you alway, *even* unto the end of the world. Amen.

This is known as the great commission, and it is our assignment. It gives us the authority to preach the Gospel worldwide. Then, the Lord told the disciples to wait in Jerusalem until they received the promise of the Father:

Acts 1:4 And, being assembled together with *them*, commanded them that they should not depart from Jerusalem, but wait for the promise of the Father, which, *saith he*, ye have heard of me.

Acts 1:8 But ye shall receive power, after that the Holy Ghost is come upon you: and ye shall be witnesses unto me both in Jerusalem, and in all Judaea, and in Samaria, and unto the uttermost part of the earth.

Notice in verse Acts 1:4 that Jesus commanded them to wait. It was not a request or just an offhand remark about hanging around in Jerusalem. They were commanded to wait so they waited in Jerusalem. They gathered and prayed in one accord. They worked on replacing Judas to complete their number once again. On Pentecost, they were gathered in one accord again:

Acts 2:1 And when the day of Pentecost was fully come, they were all with one accord in one place. 2 And suddenly there came a sound from heaven as of a rushing mighty wind, and it filled all the house where they were sitting. 3 And there appeared unto them cloven tongues like as of fire, and it sat upon each of them. 4 And they were all filled with the Holy Ghost, and began to speak with other tongues, as the Spirit gave them utterance.

This was the Baptism of the Holy Spirit and it is the watershed event in a believer's spiritual life. Before it, we are without God's dunamis power; afterward we can walk in mighty works and miracles because our Spirit has become one with the Spirit of Christ.

1 Corinthians 6:17 But he that is joined unto the Lord is one spirit.

Dunamis means power, mighty works or miracles. The baptism of the Holy Spirit is a baptism of power for service to the Lord of all creation. The fiery power that fell on those one hundred and twenty believers is what empowered them to complete the great commission. It empowered them to go into the entire world preaching the Gospel, operate in dominion over all the works of the enemy and advance the kingdom of God.

From this point on, the disciples were filled to overflowing with the power and glory of the Lord in all His fullness. People were born again, healed of all kinds of maladies and demons were cast out. People scrambled to get close to Peter because even his shadow healed all those it fell on!

The modern day church and the western church in particular are unfortunately not in complete agreement on the baptism of the Holy Spirit. There are many who believe that miracles and the gifts of the spirit died with the last apostle. Their reasoning seems sound to an analytical mind but it negates the whole area of faith rising up to help us see things that be not as though they were. It also negates or ignores all the evidence of miracles that occur on a daily basis throughout the world through spirit-filled believers. Jesus told those listening to Him to believe in the works He did if they could not believe Him:

John 10:37 If I do not the works of my Father, believe me not. 38 But if I do, though ye believe not me, believe the works: that ye may know, and believe, that the Father *is* in me, and I in him.

I was a very left brained kind of guy. I have over thirty years in the computer software industry as a software engineer and left brain thinking comes naturally to a guy like me. And, I had a lot of trouble with this whole notion in the beginning. But, seeing is believing, at least for me. And, I have seen too many miracles to ever believe that God did away with all this when the last apostle passed into eternity.

For those trained to think in the Greek[1] manner and that is most of us in the west, faith is difficult at best. Cause and effect, reasoning and a rational approach to problem solving, and anything beyond our ability to see, hear, taste or touch cannot be real and deserves no real thought. Yet, the bible teaches us that everything we see is created from things we cannot see:

2 Corinthians 4:18 While we look not at the things which are seen, but at the things which are not seen: for the things which are seen *are* temporal; but the things which are not seen *are* eternal.

Hebrews 11:3 Through faith we understand that the worlds were framed by the word of God, so that things which are seen were not made of things which do appear.

This baptism, the baptism of the Holy Spirit, is for everyone who receives Jesus as Lord. After the resurrection of our Lord, and the arrival of Pentecost, the believers received this baptism if they wanted it. Many did not – simply because they did not know what it was. But, it is for everyone who believes. Jesus did not send out the priests or professional clergy – he sent out laymen – whosoever wills.

Mark 8:34 And when he had called the people unto him with his disciples also, he said unto them, Whosoever will come after me, let him deny himself, and take up his cross, and follow me.

Again, Jesus told us he would send us another comforter and for them to wait in Jerusalem until they received power from on high:

John 14:16 And I will pray the Father, and he shall give you another Comforter, that he may abide with you for ever;

Luke 24:49 And, behold, I send the promise of my Father upon you: but tarry ye in the city of Jerusalem, until ye be endued with power from on high.

Peter said that this is that concerning the baptism and referring to Joel's prophecy:

Acts 2:14 But Peter, standing up with the eleven, lifted up his voice, and said unto them, Ye men of Judaea, and all ye that dwell at Jerusalem, be this known unto you, and hearken to my words: 15 For these are not drunken, as ye suppose, seeing it is but the third hour of the day. 16 But this is that which was spoken by the prophet Joel;

Joel 2:28 And it shall come to pass afterward, that I will pour out my spirit upon all flesh; and your sons and your daughters shall prophesy, your old men shall dream dreams, your young men shall see visions:

We need the baptism of the Holy Spirit if we are going to wage war against the enemy of our souls and prevail against him. Many today still stand opposed to this baptism and all the teaching surrounding it. But, from experience, I can tell you there is no more critical endowment from heaven needed by the spiritual warrior than the baptism of the Holy Spirit. It absolutely changes everything and we become the head rather than the tail once we receive it.

One thing I have learned over the last few years is that while men can take away or steal an idea someone has, they cannot steal an experience you have had. Once I have experienced God, no one can take that from me! Our relationship with God is supposed to be experiential which means experienced and not just head knowledge. If my only experience with God are the thoughts I give to Him as I read His word, and I never experience His supernatural power, I will be easy prey for those who are actively seeking to separate me from Him.

We experience God through His presence. God's presence can be with, in and upon a person. Again, God's presence is with us in three distinct aspects: with us, in us and upon us.

Lord Jesus please help us to know and understand how to walk in your power and might trusting you for every breath we take. Help our walk with you to be vibrant and joyous as you continue to draw us closer and closer to yourself. Give us a ravenous hunger and thirst for your Spirit so we can learn your ways and accomplish all you set us to do. In your name we pray. Amen.

The Spirit with Us

"There is no better evangelist in the world than the Holy Spirit." ~ DL Moody

The Spirit is often with people before they even know it. Even though I was not saved yet, I knew of the Lord and felt His presence with me everywhere I went, even as a youth. I now know, looking back, that the Spirit was indeed with me as He saved my life several times in the natural before I ever came to the Lord. Often times, a person may even walk in the favor of the Most High and not even know the Lord simply because someday he will know the Lord and develop a deep personal relationship with Him. We are constrained by time and space but our God is not!

The spirit-filled life is a wonderful existence and getting to know the Holy Spirit is a real joy. The personality of the Holy Spirit is like us in that He possesses emotion, a mind and a will. He performs actions consistent with a genuine and complete personality. Some of these actions include leading, consoling, teaching, interceding, bearing witness, directing and convincing. He can be obeyed, grieved, blasphemed, insulted, resisted or lied to. As a genuine person, then, He is to be distinguished from His power. He is not *an it*, some mindless force, so to speak, as some would have us believe.

But the Spirit is also fully divine, possessing all the attributes of deity. His attributes of omnipresence, omniscience, omnipotence prove that he is divine, along with the titles which are given to him, including "God." His work of creating, redeeming, and sustaining all demonstrate His divinity. Believers need to understand these truths, coupled with the fact that His advent at Pentecost inaugurated the long awaited age of the Spirit. We now live in an age where the Spirit has taken up permanent residence in the heart of the believer. His primary purpose is to reveal Christ to us and keep us safe from the enemy until the day of our glorification.

Psalms 23:4 Yea, though I walk through the valley of the shadow of death, I will fear no evil: for thou *art* with me; thy rod and thy staff they comfort me.

And, He knew us before the foundation of the world was ever set in place! Praise God!

Ephesians 1:4 According as he hath chosen us in him before the foundation of the world, that we should be holy and without blame before him in love:

Jesus told us He would never leave us nor forsake us:

Matthew 28:20 Teaching them to observe all things whatsoever I have commanded you: and, lo, I am with you alway, *even* unto the end of the world. Amen.

Hebrews 13:5 *Let your* conversation *be* without covetousness; *and be* content with such things as ye have: for he hath said, I will never leave thee, nor forsake thee.

The ministry of the Spirit is Christ-centered. It is neither man-centered with an emphasis on our gifts, personalities, and experiences, nor is the ministry of the Holy Spirit centered on Himself and His miraculous activities or ministries, as important and rich as they are. Again, the Holy Spirit calls attention to neither Himself nor to man, but focuses all attention on the Lord Jesus Christ and what God has done in and through His Son. His purpose through all His ministries is to develop our faith, hope, love, adoration, obedience, fellowship, and commitment to Jesus Christ. If the ministry you are associated with holds anyone or anything higher than Jesus, then it is not Christ-centered nor is it being Spirit led. The Holy Spirit glorifies Jesus!

Dear Holy Spirit, please help us to discern your unction at all times and help us to obey you in all love and humility. Please help us to become more sensitive to your leading every day. In the name of Jesus we pray. Amen.

The Spirit in Us

"The greatest miracle Almighty God can do is to take an unholy man out of an unholy world, make that unholy man holy, put him back in an unholy world and keep him holy! It takes all the power of the Atonement to do that, plus the indwelling of the Spirit of God and all the promises of God." ~ Leonard Ravenhill

A person that has the Spirit of God in them will be a different person than before the Spirit came to reside in them. They will be kinder, gentler, more loving and more alive than ever before. The fruit of the Spirit will be evident in his life.

The Spirit in Us

John 14:17 *Even* the Spirit of truth; whom the world cannot receive, because it seeth him not, neither knoweth him: but ye know him; for he dwelleth with you, and shall be in you.

Galatians 5:22 But the fruit of the Spirit is love, joy, peace, longsuffering, gentleness, goodness, faith, 23 Meekness, temperance: against such there is no law.

When we have His Spirit, it changes everything because now we have divine guidance, and a divine counselor who knows God's perfect will for us and can help us in every way to become all that God wants us to be. Even when we fall, we can pray and ask God to make us right:

Psalms 51:10 Create in me a clean heart, O God; and renew a right spirit within me.

God said He would put a new spirit within us and give us a heart of flesh to replace the heart of stone we had, and to help us to walk in His ways following His word. Praise God! We need all the help we can get from Him as there is so much against us in this world.

Ezekiel 11:19 And I will give them one heart, and I will put a new spirit within you; and I will take the stony heart out of their flesh, and will give them an heart of flesh:

Ezekiel 36:27 And I will put my spirit within you, and cause you to walk in my statutes, and ye shall keep my judgments, and do *them*.

Finally, we know we are His because we do have His Spirit within us. We have His word, and His promises from the Word that He would be in us and we have the down payment of all that by His Spirit.

1 John 4:13 Hereby know we that we dwell in him, and he in us, because he hath given us of his Spirit.

2 Corinthians 1:22 Who hath also sealed us, and given the earnest of the Spirit in our hearts.

2 Corinthians 5:5 Now he that hath wrought us for the selfsame thing *is* God, who also hath given unto us the earnest of the Spirit.

If we have the down payment, the earnest payment of all His promises to us in the person of the Holy Spirit who resides in us, we know we will inherit everything His word tells us! Glory! What an awesome God He is!

There is a difference between being Spirit-born (indwelling) by repenting of your sins and placing your faith in Jesus Christ as your savior and being Spirit-filled (infilling) by the Holy Spirit, where we receive the promise of Jesus Christ to live and move in power. The only condition for indwelling is the obedience of faith in Jesus Christ whereas the filling of the Spirit is dependent upon faith in the Spirit for His control.

Jack Hayford in *"living the SPIRIT FORMED LIFE,"* writes "then be Spirit-Formed by recognizing that the entry door of the new birth and the birthright blessing of Holy Spirit fullness are only beginnings – both calling us as believers to *growth* in Christ's likeness and *discipleship* under His lordship."

Dear Holy Spirit, please teach us to hear your voice clearly and help us to know all you bade us. Please draw us ever closer to Jesus and into a real intimate and personal relationship with yourself and Jesus. Help us to be spirit-filled, spirit-fed and spirit-led every moment of our lives in Jesus' name. Amen.

The Spirit upon Us

"The Holy Spirit is not a blessing from God, He is God." ~ Colin Urquhart

The Spirit upon us will cause actions and behaviors to change. The presence and glory of God will change our hearts. The power of God changes actions. The presence of the Spirit will cause us to be; the power of the Spirit will cause us to do.

1 Samuel 10:6 And the Spirit of the LORD will come upon thee, and thou shalt prophesy with them, and shalt be turned into another man.

Emotions are stirred. Power has to do with emotions. The power stirred Saul's emotions. God's presence stills us; His power stirs us.

1 Samuel 11:6 And the Spirit of God came upon Saul when he heard those tidings, and his anger was kindled greatly.

Power is released. This is most evident and described in Samson's actions as recorded in the book of Judges:

Judges 14:5 Then went Samson down, and his father and his mother, to Timnath, and came to the vineyards of Timnath: and, behold, a young lion roared against him. 6 And the Spirit of the LORD came mightily upon him, and he rent him as he would have rent a kid, and *he had* nothing in his hand: but he told not his father or his mother what he had done.

Judges 14:19 And the Spirit of the LORD came upon him, and he went down to Ashkelon, and slew thirty men of them, and took their spoil, and gave change of garments unto them which expounded the riddle. And his anger was kindled, and he went up to his father's house.

Judges 15:14 *And* when he came unto Lehi, the Philistines shouted against him: and the Spirit of the LORD came mightily upon him, and the cords that *were* upon his arms became as flax that was burnt with fire, and his bands loosed from off his hands. 15 And he found a new jawbone of an ass, and put forth his hand, and took it, and slew a thousand men therewith.

- The spirit with, in and upon us is the anointing of God.
- The anointing is given to preach the gospel to the poor
- The anointing is given to heal and restore people
- The anointing is given to proclaim freedom to the captives

- The anointing is given to open blind eyes and deaf ears
- The anointing is given to set people free
- The anointing flows in God's timing and proclaims God's timing

Acts 1:8 But ye shall receive power, after that the Holy Ghost is come upon you: and ye shall be witnesses unto me both in Jerusalem, and in all Judaea, and in Samaria, and unto the uttermost part of the earth.

1 John 2:27 But the anointing which ye have received of him abideth in you, and ye need not that any man teach you: but as the same anointing teacheth you of all things, and is truth, and is no lie, and even as it hath taught you, ye shall abide in him.

Once we receive the baptism of the Holy Spirit, we need to learn to walk in it. Pray in tongues every day. Learn to hear God's voice and anticipate that God will speak to you, daily. Find quiet time alone with Him every day and seek His will for your life. Believe that you are His child and that He loves you and will help and empower you.

Oh Lord, you are the baptizer with fire. Please fill us afresh and anew with your Holy Spirit in ever greater measure. Teach us to walk in your anointing and in power as true sons and daughters of God. Give us great faith, great boldness, great courage and great tenacity to accomplish all you set our hands to, in Jesus name. Amen.

Dead to Sin

"The greatest battles are fought in the mind." ~ Casey Treat

God defeated satan through the death and resurrection of the Lord Jesus Christ. Through this overwhelming victory, God empowers us to overcome any temptation to sin. The simple fact is that we cannot fight spiritual battles with coined phrases and secret words. We cannot overpower demons merely by shouting at them. Spiritual warfare is about destroying evil lies with the truth. Use the authority of God's Word and the power of the gospel to tell people the truth. That is what pulls down fortresses of falsehood.

The challenge before us is not merely to do what God says because He is God, but to desire what God says because He is so very, very good. We cannot just pursue righteousness, but we must prefer righteousness. If our thirst for joy, meaning and passion are satisfied by the presence of Christ, the power of sin is broken. At first lust tricks us into feeling that we would really miss out on some great satisfaction if we followed the path of purity. But then we take the sword of the Spirit and begin to fight. And as we pray for our faith to be satisfied with God's life and peace, the sword of the Spirit knocks the sugar coating off the poison of lust. And by the grace of God, lust's alluring power is broken. This is the great battle of life - to become so enamored with Jesus and so disgusted by sin that we no longer have a taste for those pleasures with which the tempter baits his hooks. We must acquire a complete distaste for all sin, because of a superior satisfaction in God.

There is a great difference between realizing Jesus was crucified for me, and that I was crucified with Him on the cross. The one aspect brings us deliverance from sin's condemnation, the other from sin's power. That old man was crucified with Jesus!

Romans 6:6 Knowing this, that our old man is crucified with *him*, that the body of sin might be destroyed, that henceforth we should not serve sin.

The reason why so many fail to overcome sin is because they wait until the hour of battle to prepare. The reason others succeed is because they gain their victory on their knees long before the battle starts. Anticipate your battles; fight them on your knees before temptation comes, and you can have victory. Anticipate where and how you will be tempted and create in your mind your reaction to those temptations. Rehearse your exit routes.

Romans 6:11 Likewise reckon ye also yourselves to be dead indeed unto sin, but alive unto God through Jesus Christ our Lord.

We must reckon ourselves to be dead to sin. If we are dead to the sin that once held us captive, we will not rise to it. No matter how firm a grip sin has on you – you will not rise to it if you are dead to it! This is an absolutely amazing truth!

Please understand that most of us do not change overnight into the person we want to become. The Bible presents salvation as a life transforming experience. And, it is! Change begins in the life of a believer in the inner core of his being as it is changed from self to a "born again" child of God. This change occurs in the very center of our lives, in our spirit. Failure to understand that this change happens in the spirit first, and then is reflected in our outward appearance through our thoughts and actions can be very confusing. The degree to which this happens is directly related to the effort we expend as we renew our minds through study of the Word of God and our obedience to the Holy Spirit's direction.

Change in the lives of Christians comes first from the inside out rather than from the soul and body inward. Suppose you were fat when you came to the Lord; you will be a fat child of God until you put your body on a weight loss regime. As our body does not change instantly, neither does our soul or mind. They must be trained in the things of God. But, remember God is well able to complete the work He has begun in us.

It is our spirit that is instantly changed at salvation. It is perfect: "the spirits of the righteous made perfect." (Heb. 12:23). The spirit does not sin: "No one who is born of God practices sin, because His seed abides in him; and he cannot sin, because he is born of God." (1Jn. 3:9) Everything that is true of Jesus is true of our born-again spirit. Our spiritual salvation is complete.

At salvation, we receive the same spirit that we will have throughout all eternity. It does not have to be changed or cleansed again. It is sealed with the Holy Spirit: "having believed, you were sealed in Him with the Holy Spirit of promise." (Eph. 1:13) and therefore, is sanctified and perfected forever: "By this will we have been sanctified through the offering of the body of Jesus Christ once for all." (Heb. 10:10) and "By one offering He has perfected for all time those who are sanctified." (Heb. 10:14)

For the rest of our Christian lives, we should not try to get faith, joy or love from God, but rather we should release what we already have in our spirits: "the fruit of the Spirit is ..." (Gal. 5:22-23) into our souls and bodies. Failure to understand this has caused some people to despair when they do not see sufficient change in their life after coming to the Lord for salvation. It must be understood that the change is internal in our spirit and the outward change occurs as we renew our minds through God's Word.

We want to overcome sin, evil and temptation in our lives and mind management is the first priority for the overcomer.

Philippians 4:8 Finally, brethren, whatsoever things are true, whatsoever things are honest, whatsoever things are just, whatsoever things are pure, whatsoever things are lovely, whatsoever things are of good report; if there be any virtue, and if there be any praise, think on these things.

For at least a year, I got up every morning and declared I was dead to sin, evil and temptation and alive in Christ Jesus; that sin, evil and temptation had no power or hold on me because I belonged to the Lord wholly and outright. The Holy Spirit led me through my wilderness and had me deal with many of the things that were wrong about me. It took some doing as I was not living righteously. After a while, the Holy Spirit had me pretty cleaned up, but I was still hanging onto a couple of addictions and a few hidden things that were even hidden from me. It would take a direct loving relationship with Jesus to set me free from all that.

I was an alcoholic and was still drinking pretty regularly though I was now saved and born again. People told me I could not really be saved and still smoke and drink like I did, but they were wrong. I was and am saved, by the grace of God – it is not about anything I did or did not do. We come to Jesus just as we are and He cleans us up. If we wait until we are clean, we will never come to Him and neither will anyone else for that matter. In fact, I could not clean myself up. I was too close to it, if you know what I mean. Some sins become part of us and we just naturally fall right into a rhythm of sinning that is so easy to continue and so easy to overlook too. There are also generational sins, and generational iniquity issues that seem to dog our heels no matter how hard we try to avoid them or abstain from them. If that is your experience, please get a copy of Neil T. Anderson's *The Bondage Breaker* and *The steps to FREEDOM IN CHRIST*, read them and apply them to your life. They will help you overcome these types of issues.

One day, I finished the last beer in the refrigerator and was getting ready to run down to the local market and get more, and my wife said "You know that God is watching you don't you?" Well, I stopped right there and thought about it. I knew God was speaking to me through my wife! I did not go to the store that day or ever since for beer or any other alcoholic product. I completely quit drinking right then and there. But, the battle was not over yet.

For the next year and a half, I got up every morning and asked God to help me not drink that day. I did not worry about tomorrow, next week, next month or next year. Just for today, "please Jesus, help me not drink today." It worked! Before I knew it, it was a month, and then three months, then a year and I had not had a drink. Praise

Dead to Sin

God!

Now, you need to understand that I come from a long line of drinkers, moonshiners and the like and this was a really, really big deal for me. At quitting time, my pickup made a beeline on its own accord for the closest convenience store for a tallboy. Jesus was faithful and he helped me overcome this terrible addiction one day at a time.

I continued to smoke cigarettes for several years after that. I had been smoking for so long and I really liked it too. I know for a fact that the last couple of years I smoked, I smoked out of sheer spite of those who gave me a hard time about it. I had people tell me "Jesus does not want you to smoke. Don't you know your body is the temple of the Holy Spirit? You must not be really saved, as no saved person could smoke cigarettes." Well, it caused me to get my back up. I was offended by all this and refused to listen to reason for a long time. The enemy had his hooks in deep and they were well planted.

Finally, I knew the Lord had had enough of this nonsense and I felt a deep, deep conviction to quit smoking altogether. My wife and I talked about it and we decided to do it together holding onto Jesus every day. So, we did the patch thing. We started with step 1, and split it between us so we were on it one week. Then, onto step 2 and we did it the same way. We split the product and were on it a week, maybe two. We prayed every day, "Jesus, please help us to not smoke this day." That worked too! After the first couple of days, I never had a real strong urge to smoke. After a meal, while driving and first thing in the morning were the tough spots for me, but Jesus was completely faithful again and He took the strong desire for smoking completely away from me. Praise God!

It does not matter what sin or addiction you are enticed by or attracted to. Its purpose is to separate you from God and from His perfect will in your life which is your destiny. It is designed to slow you down, stop your spiritual growth completely or outright kill you. Nothing good ever comes from sin or addictions. We cannot cuddle them or treat them gently either. Whatever that thing is that has us in its grip is our enemy and it is out to destroy us!

We must attack it and embarrass it or it will attack and embarrass us! If your particular weakness is a really tough one – a besetting sin or some form of addiction, then you will have to be ready to walk as close to the Lord as you possibly can in order to overcome it. Our enemy will not let go easily, nor will he stop trying to trip us up. He does not play fair and he will be merciless in his pursuit of you and your family.

John 10:10 The thief cometh not, but for to steal, and to kill, and to destroy: I am come that they might have life, and that they might have it more abundantly.

I once heard a story about a man who was hiking and fell, trapping one of his arms between two huge boulders. He hung there for days and could not free himself. All he had was a dull old pocket knife, but he used that to cut off the arm that was pinned in the boulders. Then he walked out of the wilderness until he found a road and got some help. People were astounded that he survived such an ordeal. The will to survive was strong in that man!

We too have to be willing to cut off our own arm in order to save our life! If we are not willing to do whatever it takes to overcome the sin in our lives, we will not be successful in overcoming it. Sin is not going to just go away because we want it to. You have to be willing to fight it. You have to hate it. It is your deadly mortal enemy and, I mean we really have to hate it!

Matthew 5:29 And if thy right eye offend thee, pluck it out, and cast *it* from thee: for it is profitable for thee that one of thy members should perish, and not *that* thy whole body should be cast into hell. 30 And if thy right hand offend thee, cut it off, and cast *it* from thee: for it is profitable for thee that one of thy members should perish, and not *that* thy whole body should be cast into hell.

So, study what sin entices you. Figure out how it causes you to fall into its trap. If you know what triggers the sin, you can compensate for it or avoid it. Pray and ask the Lord to help you overcome this sin, and seek out and memorize verses of scripture that deal directly with what assails you. Remember, we war from a position of victory – not towards victory – we already possess the victory! We win!

Proverbs 16:6 By mercy and truth iniquity is purged: and by the fear of the LORD *men* depart from evil.

But, to war from victory means we have to believe that we are victorious. We need to be merciful and seek the truth. The enemy will lie to us every step of the way and have us believing we cannot possibly beat this thing – whatever it is. That is a lie from the pit of hell! With Jesus, we are always victors!

The fear of the Lord is the beginning of wisdom but it is not a fear of God, it is a reverence or awe of Him and His power. He is truth and His Word is truth.

Job 28:28 And unto man he said, Behold, the fear of the Lord, that *is* wisdom; and to depart from evil *is* understanding.

Proverbs 9:10 The fear of the LORD *is* the beginning of wisdom: and the knowledge of the holy *is* understanding.

The more we know about Him and about His Word, the more understanding we will possess. If we hold God in awe, and are ever mindful of His power, His glory and His majesty we will be on the right road to overcoming the lies of the enemy.

Father God, please help to reckon ourselves dead to sin, evil and temptation; as dead as we are to our old man. Please help us to be alive to you through Jesus and in our new man so we can stand against all the things that used to entice us. Give us strength and courage to do whatever it takes to put that old man to death completely. In the name of your son, Jesus we pray. Amen.

Antidote to the Lies

What is the antidote? It is the mind of Christ; the Word of God. Who are you going to believe? Whose report are you going to believe?

1 Corinthians 2:16 For who has known the mind of the Lord, that he may instruct him? But we have the mind of Christ.

Will you believe your old programming, which is stinking thinking really, or will you believe what God says? I think it is time to come out of agreement with the enemy. It is time for you to come out of agreement with the lies you have been fed for so long. satan was and is the father of all lies. If he can get you to believe a lie, then your spirit, soul and body will conform to that image.

Isaiah 59:19 So shall they fear the name of the LORD from the west, and his glory from the rising of the sun. When the enemy shall come in like a flood, the Spirit of the LORD shall lift up a standard against him.

Hebrews 4:12 For the word of God is living, and powerful, and sharper than any two-edged sword, piercing even to the dividing asunder of soul and spirit, and of the joints and marrow, and is a discerner of the thoughts and intents of the heart.

The Word of God discerns our thoughts. At any given moment our thoughts can be from ourselves, the enemy or God. If satan can appear as an angel of light, he can appear as you to yourself. He can convince you that the garbage you have running around in your mind is you. He can speak in your voice and convince you he is you.

So, the only sane thing we can do in regard to our thoughts is to know what God has to say about a subject. We should not get caught up in our minds with precepts, concepts, thoughts and realities that do not line up with the Word of God. How can we measure what comes into our minds unless our minds are washed clean? We need to wash our minds daily with the Word of God, and pray in tongues.

Ephesians 5:26 That he might sanctify and cleanse it with the washing of water by the word,

John 15:3 Now ye are clean through the word which I have spoken unto you.

If we do that, feed our Spirit man with the Word of God daily and wash and subject our minds to God's way of thinking and His truth, we can reprogram our minds back to what God intended. That is step one of this process. We need to proceed and then take every thought captive that enters our minds.

2 Corinthians 10:5 Casting down arguments, and every high thing that exalts itself against the knowledge of God, and bringing into captivity every thought to the obedience of Christ;

We must take every thought and measure it against the Word of God. If it is of God, then it can stay. Otherwise, cast it out! If a thought does not agree with God's Word, then you must cast it down and out of your mind. Our will is stronger than our emotions and we can force ourselves to avoid certain things we know cause us trouble. Sin always begins in our minds. We must bring every thought into obedience to the mind of Christ!

If we are His, we do have the mind of Christ. Again, our thoughts come from one of three places – from ourselves, from the enemy or from God. We must take every thought captive – do not allow your thoughts free reign in you. Bring every thought that enters your mind to the front and measure it against the Word of God. If it is of God, then it can remain. If not, cast it out in the name of Jesus.

<u>You must get this – every sin begins in our minds!</u> If a thought is not of God, and we entertain it, dwell on it or give it full access to us – we will fall and succumb to it. We have to be very practical in

this regard and not allow our guard to drop. Every thought must be brought into captivity and measured against the Word of God! This is critical!

2 Corinthians 10:5 Casting down imaginations, and every high thing that exalteth itself against the knowledge of God, and bringing into captivity every thought to the obedience of Christ;

Jesus did not sin therefor the enemy had no place in Him – satan could not entice or lure Him into sin no matter how subtle the temptation might have been. This is because the enemy had no place in Him! If we allow the enemy free access to our thought life, we are in for big trouble.

John 8:46 Which of you convinceth me of sin? And if I say the truth, why do ye not believe me?

John 14:30 Hereafter I will not talk much with you: for the prince of this world cometh, and hath nothing in me.

Keep your eyes focused on Jesus. Always! If you fall, analyze why you fell so you can be better prepared the next time that situation or circumstance occurs. Then, commit to not falling to that sin in the same way ever again. Some people like to confront their sins and face them down (with the help of the Holy Spirit of course), and others must learn to avoid the triggering mechanisms that cause them to sin. Which way is right? Only you and the Lord know what is right for you. Whatever works for you to be able to stand strong and abstain from that sin is the right way in your case. But ask God and He will provide a way to escape:

1 Corinthians 10:13 There hath no temptation taken you but such as is common to man: but God *is* faithful, who will not suffer you to be tempted above that ye are able; but will with the temptation also make a way to escape, that ye may be able to bear *it*.

The Lord will *always* provide a way of escape from sin, evil and temptation. In order to see the avenue of escape, we have to be actively looking for it. It is not going to chase us down and say go this way! In order to become an over-comer, we need total surrender to God and absolute loyalty to Him above everything else. Our arm or our life - we must be willing to cut off every addictive behavior and live! Cut off all contact with people, places and things that cause us to sin.

We cannot change where we have come from, but we can change where we are going and how we will travel that road! This is a battle we will face all the days of our lives while we remain on this earth. We must learn where we are weak and where we are strong and live accordingly and consistently, holding onto Jesus tightly every step of the way.

Oh Lord of all creation, please help us to attain the mind of Christ so we can cast down everything that exalts itself against you. Help us to keep our eyes focused on Jesus and not allow the ways and wiles of this world to lure us off course. In the precious name of Jesus I pray. Amen.

Help Me! I have Fallen

"Fallen man is not simply an imperfect creature who needs improvement: he is a rebel who must lay down his arms." ~ C.S. Lewis

Ok, so what do you do if you overcome the sin that was tempting you, and later you fall either partly or completely right back into it? You pick yourself up, confess your sin to God and ask for His forgiveness. Always remember, God wants to forgive us. We do not have to twist His arm or beg Him to forgive us as this is who He is.

Psalms 36:5 Thy mercy, O LORD, *is* in the heavens; *and* thy faithfulness *reacheth* unto the clouds.

Psalms 106:1 Praise ye the LORD. O give thanks unto the LORD; for he is good: for his mercy endureth for ever.

1 John 1:9 If we confess our sins, he is faithful and just to forgive us *our* sins, and to cleanse us from all unrighteousness.

This last verse is known as the Christian's bar of soap. Use it liberally and literally, on a daily basis so you can keep a really short list of offenses between you and God. If we confess our sins, He will wash us clean. I do this daily. If I can remember anything I said or did that may in any way be offensive to man or God, I use the Christian's bar of soap to get right with God. The enemy wants us to allow sin to come between us and God, and we can short circuit that by being really quick to confess anything and everything. Believe me, when you confess this sin (whatever it is), that will not be the first time God hears about it! He already knew you'd do that and He stands ready, even eager to forgive. What an awesome God He is!

Remember, it is not a sin to be tempted. I used to hear people say "well, I might as well do it since I thought about it." But, that is just not true. Jesus was tempted in all things just like we are.

Hebrews 4:15 For we have not an high priest which cannot be touched with the feeling of our infirmities; but was in all points tempted like as *we are, yet* without sin.

But, He never sinned! So, being tempted and sinning are two distinct and separate events. Do not allow the enemy to talk you into sinning just because you were tempted. Actually, a lot of our training as warriors has to do with learning how to avoid sin and step away from the temptation. Even if we cannot do so physically, we can step away in our mind. We need to make up our mind that we will not succumb to that sin any more, and we will do whatever it takes to stick to that conviction.

Galatians 2:19 For I through the law am dead to the law, that I might live unto God. 20 I am crucified with Christ: nevertheless I live; yet not I, but Christ lives in me: and the life which I now live in the flesh I live by the faith of the Son of God, who loved me, and gave himself for me.

We can overcome every sin that besets us! We have the mind of Christ and we can bring every thought into obedience. Further, when we accepted Jesus and were baptized, we were crucified with Him and therefore we are dead to sin, evil and temptation. Those are the facts from the Word of God! Believe them!

Meditate on this simple statement: "I am dead to sin and alive to Jesus Christ." Repeat it under your breath throughout your day to day activity. Say it out loud whenever you are tempted. Use every opportunity to get this simple yet life-changing principle ingrained in your mind. When that familiar temptation comes up again, you may feel the same but God's power to overcome is available to you. Face it with the statement "I am dead to sin and alive to Jesus Christ."

Father, I thank You for delivering me from all the power of sin. Please help me learn to lean on Your strength whenever I am battling temptation. In Jesus' name I pray. Amen.

Walking in the Spirit

"The preaching that this world needs most is the sermons in shoes that are walking with Jesus Christ." ~ DL Moody

One of the real keys to living a life above the snake line involves a process known as walking in the spirit. The Word tells us we will not fulfill the lusts of the flesh if we are walking in the spirit.

Galatians 5:16 This I say then, Walk in the Spirit, and you shall not fulfill the lust of the flesh.

Galatians 5:25 If we live in the Spirit, let us also walk in the Spirit.

So, what does it mean to walk in the spirit? This is a daily choice we make to seek the ways of God above and beyond what we feel like doing, or what the world deems as normal religious behavior. The key points involved in walking in the spirit include:

- dependence upon the spirit
- obedience to the spirit
- keeping in step with the spirit
- availability to the spirit - this is the secret to abiding
- friendship with the spirit

If we do this on a daily basis, we can expect the results to be awesome and wonderful:

- complete deliverance from sin
- peace - serenity, tranquility and steadfastness
- providences - something God chooses for us and promotes
- great blessings - to every life fully surrendered

A key point in learning to walk in the Spirit is seeking hard after God on a daily basis. Reading the Bible every day should be a priority for all of us. Also, we should seek to remain in the presence of God at all times. There is a little book by Brother Lawrence called *Practicing the Presence of God* that talks about this. Basically, that involves bringing God to mind frequently and not allowing ourselves to go too long without giving Him thought.

Walking in the Spirit involves two things: putting to death the desires of the flesh, and choosing to follow and obey God. As you say no to sin and yes to the Holy Spirit, you will discover the meaning of true freedom. When we sin, we need to be quick to confess and repent of that and draw close to God again. If we stay constant in prayer which is communion with God, it is easier to walk in the Spirit.

Ephesians 6:18 Praying always with all prayer and supplication in the Spirit, and watching thereunto with all perseverance and supplication for all saints;

Romans 12:12 Rejoicing in hope; patient in tribulation; continuing instant in prayer;

Dear heavenly Father, thank You for equipping me to serve You through the gift of grace. Help me die to my selfish desires and ambitions and obediently submit to Your will for my life. In the name of Jesus I pray. Amen.

Time Daily with Jesus

"Closet communion needs time for the revelation of God's presence. It is vain to say, 'I have too much work to do to find time.' You must find time or forfeit blessing. God knows how to save for you the time you sacredly keep for communion with Him." ~ A.T. Pierson

John 15:4 Abide in me, and I in you. As the branch cannot bear fruit of itself, except it abide in the vine; no more can ye, except ye abide in me.

John 15:6 If a man abide not in me, he is cast forth as a branch, and is withered; and men gather them, and cast *them* into the fire, and they are burned. 7 If ye abide in me, and my words abide in you, ye shall ask what ye will, and it shall be done unto you.

The Lord usually wakes me with a song in my heart (spirit) every morning. This has occurred daily for at least the last seven years. When I feel Him rousing me, I get up immediately. If The Lord of all creation wakes me, I am getting up! He often wakes me earlier than I planned on getting up and sometimes He wakes me with a real burden to pray on my heart. Other times, He just wants to fellowship with me. What a privilege! What an honor to be so loved and cherished by the Lord. But, this is not just for a few! It can be your experience too! My priorities as I start each day are:

Father, help us to know and understand how important daily time with you in your presence is for our growth, in Jesus' name. Amen.

1st Priority - Jesus Time

"There is always time to look up to Him for His smile." ~ F. B. Meyer

I start my day with the Lord – every day. This is the most amazing and rewarding experience of my life and my Christian walk as it bears more fruit than anything else I have ever done to draw close to Him. The Lord wants a close personal relationship with each one of us. And, that is exactly what we need too even if we are not aware of it. All we have to do is seek Him.

Luke 11:9 And I say unto you, Ask, and it shall be given you; seek, and ye shall find; knock, and it shall be opened unto you.

We definitely need daily time with the Lord – to draw close to Him, to learn His ways, to build up our spirit and our anointing, and to maintain our walk in the Spirit. We should seek Him early each day before we are faced with the latest crisis, complaint or problem. I had an old Mexican vaquero tell me once that he thanked God for another day to live each day before he even opened his eyes each morning. His first thought and prayer was to God! You know God loved this man!

Proverbs 8:17 I love them that love me; and those that seek me early shall find me.

We can start fresh with God every single day, just by seeking Him out, reading His word, praising Him, worshiping Him and waiting on Him.

Lamentations 3:21 This I recall to my mind, therefore have I hope. 22 *It is of* the LORD'S mercies that we are not consumed, because his compassions fail not. 23 *They are* new every morning: great *is* thy faithfulness. 24 The LORD *is* my portion, saith my soul; therefore will I hope in him. 25 The LORD *is* good unto them that wait for him, to the soul *that* seeketh him.

What an amazing and wonderful God our Lord is! He wants fellowship with us and He will do everything He can to draw us to Himself so that can happen. I start my day with greeting the Lord, "Good morning Lord, I love you!" Then, I worship and praise Him for a bit, then I journal the previous day or series of day's events. Then, I pray or study if I am in that mode at that time. Then, I read

His word and pray His word over myself and my family. This will take me from an hour and a half to two hours on a daily basis. Some will think this is an awfully long time, but it flies by for me and I have to be careful not to forget my time limits and other responsibilities. As I said – this is my most productive and rewarding time and it is easy to get caught up in it and forget my schedule.

Speaking of a schedule, you must schedule time with the Lord every day. If you do not, you will not be able to find time to do it. The enemy will use every possible distraction to preempt your Jesus time if you allow him to do that. He is completely set against us having a personal relationship with the Lord, and will use every wile in his arsenal to sidetrack you in this most important step. So, set a time each and every day where you will not allow interruptions to impede your progress with the Lord. Do not turn on the television, or the radio, or check email. Keep this time special, especially for you and Jesus. I do my time with Jesus the first thing every morning before the children are awake or there would not be any time for it! I have been doing this for the last fifteen years or so now.

Oh Lord, you who dwell above the circle of the earth and know the hearts and minds of all men, please help me to make time in my busy life to spend quality time in your presence each and every day. Please help me arrange my schedule so I can draw closer to you, to Jesus and to the Holy Spirit. Teach me your ways Father. In Jesus' name I pray. Amen

2nd Priority - The Word

"A thorough knowledge of the Bible is worth more than a college education." ~ Theodore Roosevelt

One day, I was telling one of my sons about the awesome power of God's word and how important it was to fill ourselves with it daily.

2nd Priority – The Word

His response to me was "Do I have to think about God every day?" I was floored. I responded "Why, yes, of course you should think about God every day. He wakes you every morning – try getting up without being awakened." He gives us every breath we take. Scripture tells us we can do nothing – that is NO THING, without him!

John 15:5 I am the vine, ye *are* the branches: He that abideth in me, and I in him, the same bringeth forth much fruit: for without me ye can do nothing.

The Word of God is the food of our Spirit Man. Without daily doses of our spiritual food, our spirit-man will grow weaker and weaker. If we are to face the hordes of hell and stand against them, we need all the strength we can get. Do not despise the Word of God. He has gone to great lengths to preserve His Word against all kinds of attacks – which still continue to this day. There is nothing written anywhere in this world that can compare to the Word of God.

In jail, they use an acronym for the Bible: BIBLE – Basic Instructions Before Leaving Earth. How appropriate! That is exactly what it is! If you want to know God, you must read His word as He reveals Himself to us primarily through His word. As I said earlier, our Spirits crave God's Word and without it, our spirit man will begin to shrivel up and shrink in size as he is preempted by our flesh and our soul. The goal is for our spirit man to rule us. We are to walk in the spirit – that is the only way to avoid the lust of the flesh:

Galatians 5:16 This I say then, Walk in the Spirit, and you shall not fulfill the lust of the flesh.

Galatians 5:25 If we live in the Spirit, let us also walk in the Spirit.

I can go on and on about this subject, so suffice it to say if you want to become a true man or woman of God – you must immerse yourself in His Word. There is no other way to draw near and learn

His ways. And, we desperately need to learn His ways if we are to wage war against the enemies of our souls. Remember, Jesus is the Word become flesh:

John 1:14 And the Word was made flesh, and dwelt among us, (and we beheld his glory, the glory as of the only begotten of the Father,) full of grace and truth.

What an awesome picture of our Lord! He is the Word of God! When we spend time in the Word, we are spending time with Jesus. The more time we spend with Jesus, the more like Him we will become!

Occasionally, I will have a verse of scripture just drop into my heart without warning or provocation. I know this is something the Lord does to get my attention and direct my efforts, so I study that verse. I look up all the cross references and double-check it against my Thompson Chain Reference. I also check it against Commentaries and the Treasury of Scripture Knowledge in my SwordSearcher Bible software. I want to ensure I have a thorough understanding of that Word because the Lord does not do this just for fun. He has a reason for it and I want to be prepared.

The Lord does this for me in preparation for some ministry that is coming up (often, before I even know about it) or something that might be weighing on my mind that I am not totally in tune with as yet. This is a marvelous phenomenon and it excites me every time He does it. I know the Lord likes for us to anticipate His activity in our lives. It builds our faith.

My recommendation is to read at least five to six chapters a day. I read the chapter of Proverbs for whatever day of the month it is (if today is the 5th of September, I would read the 5th chapter of Proverbs), one chapter from any of the four Gospels (Matthew, Mark, Luke and John), one or two chapters from Psalms, one chapter from the Old Testament and One chapter from the New Testament. This will take less than thirty minutes and will feed your spirit-man well.

If you are a slow reader, start with Proverbs and a chapter from one of the four Gospels. Do not read hurriedly. Take your time and think about what you are reading and how it relates to your life. Let the Word dwell in you. There are a lot of theories about how to interpret scripture. My theory is just let it come to you literally. If it says "love the Lord with all your heart and soul, with all your mind and all your might," then that is exactly what it means.

One final note on this topic – always pray before you read and ask the Holy Spirit to help you stay focused and to help you to understand His word. After all, He is the author of it and only He can interpret the Word exactly as He intends for us to interpret it. Here is a sample prayer like one I use every day:

Psalms 119:169 Let my cry come near before thee, O LORD: give me understanding according to thy word.

Dear heavenly Father, I thank you for the wonder of your Word which is more than food and drink to me, it is life and medicine to my body, soul and spirit. Come Holy Spirit, come and open my spiritual eyes and reveal the wonder of your Word unto me. Please help me to know and understand your Word and let it dwell in me richly. Please protect me and my mind from any attacks from the enemy to interfere with my study this morning. In Jesus' name I pray. Amen.

3rd Priority – Prayer

"Heaven does not come to earth cheap. It never has! It takes prayer." ~ Norvel Hayes

"It seems God is limited by our prayer life - that He can do nothing for humanity unless someone asks Him." ~ John Wesley

If you are a spirit filled believer in the Lord Jesus Christ, then you must find time to pray in tongues every day. As we discussed earlier, this edifies you. It builds up your spirit-man and will increase the level and power of the anointing of God in your life. Most recommendations I have heard say to pray at least one hour a day, every day. Personally, I do not set a timer, or watch a clock. I pray as I am led to pray. Often, this is broken up by my daily activities and I pray and sing in the Spirit as the Spirit leads me as I go about my business. There is rarely a moment when a song is not near to my lips. Scripture says, "Rejoice in the Lord always, again I say rejoice!"

Philippians 4:4 Rejoice in the Lord alway: and again I say, Rejoice.

There are so many examples of God's goodness and grace demonstrated to us each and every day. I nearly always break out praising Him in tongues or spiritual singing when I see His hand at work. It really thrills me and the spirit within me leaps and praises God!

On another line of thought, I have heard people all my life say I did not know what to do, or I tried everything I could think of and nothing helped, so then I prayed. We have this all backwards. Prayer should not be the last thing we do – it should be the first thing we do! Prayer is our number one weapon as there is no time or distance in the Spirit. I can pray for anyone, anywhere and God can and will step into that situation for that person and change things! One key thing to remember is that oftentimes, we have not because we ask not:

James 4:2 You lust, and have not: you kill, and desire to have, and cannot obtain: you fight and war, yet you have not, because you ask not.

Prayer is awesome! God answers prayer. He always has and He always will. I have received the answer to my prayers so quickly that it astounded me. I have had God answer before I finished the prayer! Our Father loves us – immensely and intensely! He will always answer us if we believe His Word and believe the best about Him. He is bigger, better and more awesome than we can

3rd Priority – Prayer

imagine. And, nothing moves Him to act on our behalf like prayer does.

Matthew 7:7 Ask, and it shall be given you; seek, and you shall find; knock, and it shall be opened unto you: 8 For every one that asks receives; and he that seeks finds; and to him that knocks it shall be opened. 9 Or what man is there of you, whom if his son ask bread, will he give him a stone? 10 Or if he ask a fish, will he give him a serpent? 11 If you then, being evil, know how to give good gifts unto your children, how much more shall your Father who is in heaven give good things to them that ask him?

Right after I was saved, I would spend an incredible amount of time thinking about the things the Lord has given me and done for me in my life and I would thank Him and praise Him for each one in prayer. I could literally spend a couple of hours a day just thanking God for all He has done and is doing in my life, as well as for those attributes of His that He continually displays to me.

I am so blessed it is hard to describe to anyone else just how much the Lord has blessed me. I honestly believe I am one of the most blessed people on earth. The Lord has literally given me everything I have ever asked for or dreamed of. He has blessed me packed down, shaken about and overflowing; and, it is still in progress! He loves to bless His children and He blesses us so we can bless others. All of this puts me in a mindset that causes me to praise God at every opportunity and thank him for His marvelous works. I arise in the morning praising and thanking Him and I go to sleep at night praising and thanking Him.

When I think about the attributes of God, and how much He has taught me about Himself, I am awed and again, I feel a compelling need to praise Him and thank Him. He is utterly faithful and will never fail us. He is absolutely good every day in every aspect of His nature. He is generous and loves to give gifts to men. He is full of mercy and His mercies are new every morning. He is Holy, beyond anything we can imagine. He is deserving of all our praise!

Ephesians 4:8 Wherefore he saith, When he ascended up on high, he led captivity captive, and gave gifts unto men.

I said all that to say prayer is two way communications with the Lord. We should not just run through a list of the things we need or want. We should begin by praising God for who He is to us. Then, we can lay petitions at His feet and wait for His reply. God will answer us and He does not hold things back from us. Sometimes the answer is no for very good reasons and sometimes the answer is not immediately because God waits for the best time to deliver His best for us. There is good, better and best and we need to learn to be mature and patient enough to wait for His best.

There are different types of prayer: prayers of adoration and thanksgiving, prayers of intercession, prayers of supplication and prayers for spiritual warfare to name a few. Most of us tend to jump right into the supplication mode every time we begin praying. I think there is a better way we should consider. As I said earlier, God does not withhold things from us trying to make us earn them or become worthy of them. He is generous in all His ways and loves to give gifts to men. But, He will not give us something that will harm us. God is always good and always does exactly the right thing. Always!

Prayers of Adoration and Thanksgiving

These types of prayer should be offered up to God throughout our day in an attitude of gratitude and love for God. It is also our praise of God for all He has and is doing in our lives and it is the thanksgiving prayers we offer to Him in response to that. Psalm 100 is a perfect picture of how we should approach God in prayer:

Psalms 100:1 A Psalm of praise. Make a joyful noise unto the LORD, all ye lands. 2 Serve the LORD with gladness: come before his presence with singing. 3 Know ye that the LORD he *is* God: *it is* he *that* hath made us, and not we ourselves; *we are* his people, and the sheep of his pasture. 4 Enter into his gates with thanksgiving, *and* into his courts with praise: be thankful unto him,

3rd Priority – Prayer

and bless his name. 5 For the LORD *is* good; his mercy *is* everlasting; and his truth *endureth* to all generations.

Get that? We enter His gates with thanksgiving and into His courts with praise. When we praise Him, He shows up! This becomes our private worship of all God is for us as we thank Him and praise Him. He is certainly worthy of all our praise and thanksgiving. I nearly always begin every prayer by praising and/or thanking God for His wonderful works in my life.

I start my day and most meetings or training sessions with prayer that honors God and asks for His favor in my day, or in the meeting or training session I am participating in. Again, the bible tells us we have not because we ask not.

Prayer is one of our key weapons and we need to hone and sharpen this ability and skill faithfully. We should not waste time praying for things just so we can consume them (upon our lusts as the King James declares).

Prayers of Intercession

Oftentimes, the Lord wakes me with a burden to pray, but I do not know what it is I am to pray for, so I pray in the spirit (pray in tongues) until I feel a release. This occurs fairly frequently and I believe it is important to drop what we are doing and pray in the Spirit as we are led. I also maintain a list of people or situations I am currently praying for and will go over that list and pray for those on the list. Finally, I pray for anyone else the Lord brings to my mind during this time as I am convinced that is how He prompts me to pray.

I will also pray for anyone that pops into my head throughout the day. I know the Lord works this way, at least with me in that He will bring people to my mind I have not thought about in years or someone I just met but perhaps do not know very well. This is how the Lord leads me to intercede for others and I know it is very effective and produces great fruit.

I have had a lot of people ask me if it is ok to pray for something or someone more than once. I think we need to be led by the Holy Spirit, and if I feel a need to pray for a situation or a person more than once I listen to the Spirit and pray. I do not think there are set formulas that work every time or give us the best results. Every time we put God in a box – it is too small! There is another acronym I have seen called PUSH, Prayer until Something Happens. Jesus told a parable about a widow who persisted in presenting her case before a judge until she wore the judge down and he answered her petition:

Luke 18:1 And he spake a parable unto them *to this end*, that men ought always to pray, and not to faint; 2 Saying, There was in a city a judge, which feared not God, neither regarded man: 3 And there was a widow in that city; and she came unto him, saying, Avenge me of mine adversary. 4 And he would not for a while: but afterward he said within himself, Though I fear not God, nor regard man; 5 Yet because this widow troubleth me, I will avenge her, lest by her continual coming she weary me.

So, Jesus Himself told us to persist in prayer and not to grow faint in doing so. Why would I want to contradict Jesus? There is also the concept of praying through a situation. This is when we pray about something until something happens, or we sense in the spirit that we have our petition. That means that we sense that God will do what we have asked Him for, that in fact we know that we have our answer and there is no longer any need for that particular prayer. Or, we sense the answer is no or not now. If we sense this, then we should stop and honor God. He is sovereign.

Prayers of Supplication

These are the prayers where we ask the Lord for something in our life or for someone else. It can be a better job, a spouse, peace in our hearts or peace in the world. These prayers (also known as petitioning) are the most common form of prayer, where a person asks God to provide something, either for the person who is praying or for someone else on whose behalf a prayer of

3rd Priority – Prayer

supplication is being made.

<u>Spiritual Warfare</u>

Have you ever played a game not knowing the rules? Imagine you are playing a football game, without understanding the rules. You might find yourself asking questions like these. What do you do with the ball? Why are these players hitting me? You may quit or simply lie on the ground in agony, not understanding why the other team hit you. This is what happens in the spiritual realm, when someone comes to Jesus Christ, and is born again. Many times the new Christian finds himself in the middle of a war, not understanding why he is under attack or how to defend himself.

Once we become a Christian, we are in a war whether we know it or not. Our enemy is very real and he is going to come against us just because we are now outside of his kingdom. The Bible tells us there is an invisible realm which is distinct from our physical realm. Our physical world is in many ways under the power of this spiritual world. Most of the evil in the world is a direct result of this unseen war. The number of personalities involved in this conflict is staggering. They involve both the forces of satan composed of fallen angels and of God along with His angels. This battle is played out in our realm, in the physical world.

1 Peter 5:8 Be sober, be vigilant; because your adversary the devil, as a roaring lion, walketh about, seeking whom he may devour:

According to scripture, the targets of this battle are the souls of men, and the battlefield where all this takes place is in the mind of man, blinding us from the truth, so that we perish without salvation. We need to understand that the root behind the conflict is not physical, but spiritual. The angelic and demonic conflicts are being played out in physical realms which involve us.

When we receive thoughts about doubt and unbelief, guilt, self-abasement and self-hatred we need to understand who the source is. Since the Word says God has not given us a spirit of fear and we find fear in our life, then we must do warfare against it. When thoughts like "God does not love me" overrun our minds, then we need to cast them down. Let God be true and everyman a liar.

Romans 3:4 God forbid: yea, let God be true, but every man a liar; as it is written, That thou mightest be justified in thy sayings, and mightest overcome when thou art judged.

One aspect of spiritual warfare is understanding and declaring who we are in Christ Jesus, by reciting His promises and affirmations to us. We declare His Word back to Him as we recite His promises to us. It is very hard to be strong in the Spirit if we do not believe we are strong or mighty in the Spirit. God honors faith and we build up our faith by declaring who we are by reciting those verses the Lord has quickened to us. Here are some of the verses that are worthy of daily decree. So, pick the ones that speak to you and recite them over yourself until you believe them (also listed as Appendix B):

- Nothing can separate me from God's love (Romans 8:39).
- I am a child of God (John 1:12; Romans 8:16).
- Jesus is my Lord, Savior, and friend (1 Corinthians 12:3).
- I am born again of the Spirit (John 3:3,7; 1 Peter 1:23).
- I am a new creation; old things have passed away (2 Corinthians 5:17).
- I am saved by His grace, through faith (Ephesians 2:8-9).
- I have an immutable covenant with the Creator, sworn by Himself (Hebrews 6:13-20).
- That covenant is ratified in His own blood (Mark 14:24).
- I am blessed (Psalm 1:1).
- I am Abraham's seed (2 Corinthians 11:22).
- I have the blessing of Abraham (Galatians 3:14).
- I am blessed with every spiritual blessing in heavenly places in Christ (Ephesians 1:3).
- My wife of noble character is my crown (Proverbs 12:4,).
- My children are blessed (Proverbs 20:7).

3rd Priority – Prayer

- My descendants will be mighty on the earth (Psalm 112:2).
- I have an abundant life (John 10:10).
- God filled and empowered me with His Spirit (Acts 1:8).
- I was chosen in Him before the foundation of the world (Ephesians 1:4).
- God predestined me, called me, justified me, and will glorify me (Romans 8:30).
- All my sins are forgiven (Psalm 103:3a).
- He heals all my diseases (Psalm 103:3b).
- He causes me to prosper and be in health (Proverbs 10:22).
- I am rich (2 Corinthians 8:9).
- I can do all things through Christ who strengthens me (Philippians 4:13).
- I am a joint heir with Christ (Romans 8:17).
- It is the Father's good pleasure to give me the kingdom (Luke 12:32).
- If I believe it, speak it, and do not doubt it, I can move mountains (Mark 11:23).
- Things I pray for, if I believe I receive them, I shall have them (Mark 11:24).
- As He is, so am I in this world (1 John 4:17).
- He supplies all my needs according to His riches in glory (Philippians 4:19).
- No evil shall come upon me, nor shall any sickness come near my house (Psalm 91:10).
- He gives His angels charge over me (Psalm 91:11).
- An angel encamps all around me (Psalm 34:7).
- I am strong in the Lord and in the power of His might (Ephesians 6:10).
- He has given me authority over all the power of Satan (Luke 10:19).
- Nothing Satan does can hurt me (Luke 10:19).
- I cast out demons (Mark 16:17).
- I lay hands on the sick and they shall recover (Mark 16:18).
- God causes all things to work together for my good

(Romans 8:28).
- Christ is my wisdom, righteousness, sanctification, and redemption (1 Corinthians 1:30).
- He is my peace (Ephesians 2:14).
- I fear no evil, for He is with me (Psalm 23:4).
- I am not afraid of evil reports; my heart is steadfast, trusting in the Lord (Psalm 112:7).
- Jesus has gone to prepare a place for me (John 14:2).
- Eye has not seen nor ear heard what God has prepared for me (1 Corinthians 2:9).
- He will satisfy me with long life (Psalm 91:16).
- Goodness and mercy shall follow me all the days of my life (Psalm 23:6).
- When I leave my body, I will be present with the Lord, forever (2 Corinthians 5:8).
- If He returns before I die, I will meet Him in the air, maybe soon (1 Thessalonians 4:17).

We will discuss spiritual warfare again in even greater depth in Volume Two, *Discerning Enemy Activity*.

The enemy will attack us in our mind, in our work, in our families, and in our churches until we really come to understand who we are in Jesus Christ, the Anointed One. Once that happens, he is more likely to attack another believer who does not know who they are in Christ.

A good friend of mine, John Carrette, who is the International Executive Vice President for the United States of America, of the Full Gospel Business Men's Fellowship, International told me a story about a 2nd Lieutenant who went to Vietnam right out of Officer Candidate School. When he arrived, he met the Platoon Sergeant who was running the platoon. He asked him to please just watch, listen and learn for a couple of weeks before he did anything or made any command decisions as the man he was replacing was going out on the medical evacuation chopper that

3rd Priority – Prayer

just left. John thought it over and agreed.

So, for a few weeks, he did just that. The Sergeant was very, very good and was deeply concerned about his men and John learned quite a lot from him. One day, a colonel from headquarters showed up. The colonel told him he was killing the war effort. John said "no way, you are responsible for a lot more men that I am so you must be killing the war effort." The colonel asked him what his first priority was when he went out on patrol. John did not even have to think about it – he answered "get my men back in one piece without suffering any causality." The colonel asked him if was suffering any losses and he had to admit he was – mostly through slow attrition – sniper fire. The enemy seemed to dog their heels and take one here and two there.

The colonel said "I know a way to stop all that." John was interested and listened very carefully. The colonel told him the enemy was after them because they had assumed a defensive posture and as long as they were on the defensive, the enemy would continue to pick off one here and two there. The way to stop all that was to take the battle to the enemy. If he would go out, seek out the enemy and destroy him wherever he found him, the attrition rate would slow down and cease before long. Why should the enemy incur losses fighting a ferocious foe when he could safely pick off the stragglers and other easy targets of an enemy who did not bring the fight to him?

John went back and talked with the Sergeant about all this. He thought about it for quite a while and came to the conclusion that the colonel was right. So, they made plans to alter their approach and from that day on, they took the fight to the enemy. The attrition rate slowed and then stopped altogether. They were a force to be reckoned with and the enemy knew it and avoided them. From that day on until he rotated back to the United States, he lost very few of his men.

This is exactly what we have to do. We must take the battle to the enemy because he is picking off our stragglers, our family members and our weakest members because we have circled the wagons and are just trying to hold them off. When we take the battle to him, he will be on the defensive and will not have the inclination to come against us like he has in the past.

How do we take the battle to him? We fight evil with good. We do the right thing in every situation and we help everyone we encounter in our walk. We pray for the sick, for the demonized, for the bound and we help them see the light so they can be set free too. We declare the majesty and glory of our God and we honor Him in everything we do. We worship Him in Spirit and in truth. We act like true sons and daughters of God, Most High!

Abba, please teach me to pray with fervor and with my whole heart in ways that are pleasing to you. Teach me to spend more time with you in communion through prayer and make me a man of prayer. Help me to pray your will Father and not just my own selfish desires. In Jesus name I pray. Amen.

4th Priority – Journaling

"The gospel is not speculation but fact. It is truth, because it is the record of a Person who is the Truth." ~ Alexander MacLaren

1 Chronicles 16:4 And he appointed certain of the Levites to minister before the ark of the LORD, and to record, and to thank and praise the LORD God of Israel:

John 1:34 And I saw, and bare record that this is the Son of God.

On nearly a daily basis, I get my journal out and record the Lord's work and activities in my life since my last journal entry. I really do try and journal daily but sometimes I cannot so I do it as often as I can. This too is very rewarding in that I can see His hand in my life on a daily basis and in so many small details. It truly is mind boggling that the Lord can manage all of our affairs and schedules and coordinate all the events of billions of lives simultaneously with no effort at all on His part. In fact, I am convinced He loves to do this and that when we hand over even the small details of our lives to Him, He enjoys making them work out in our best interest.

Romans 8:28 And we know that all things work together for good to them that love God, to them who are the called according to his purpose.

One thing that is really important to make note of here is that if we do not record the Lord's activity and His answers to our prayers, we will soon forget them. We may remember the really big ones, but even then we will lose most of the details. The way our lives move from one crisis or event to another and the way we learn and grow will cause this is happen. If you really want mountain moving faith, then you need to be able to see His hand in your life; regularly!

I record prayers, answers to prayers, divine intervention through healing and deliverance, words of knowledge and words of wisdom He gives me through His Holy Spirit, prophesies, attacks and tactics of the enemy against me, my family and my ministry and all other divine communication from the Lord. This is a detailed picture of a finely woven tapestry that is called my life with God and it truly is remarkable in its height, depth and breadth. He is in everything and touches everything in our lives! I never really understood how much this was true until I started recording it in a journal. When I go back and re-read the entries in my journals, it amazes me how faithful and complete the instructions are from the Lord as He leaves nothing out of this tapestry. I can see the answers to every prayer, especially those that are harder to discern when they occur. Specifically, prayers like "Lord, please help me to walk in your Spirit each day." When I go back and re-read those sections following such a prayer, it is astounding how complete the answer is from the Lord. Sometimes, it is so subtle that it could not be noticed in any other way.

Finally, I also learned to hear God through my journaling. A lot of what follows comes from being able to hear God and I will go into the details of how that works for me next under Hearing God below.

Dear heavenly Father, please teach me to record my life and my experiences with you. Help me to see clearly how intimately you are working in my life and how detailed are your works that sustain and nurture me. Please reveal the leading of the Holy Spirit in my life and make this so very real to me that I will never ever forget your love and wonderful care of me. In the name of your son, Jesus I pray. Amen.

Hearing God

"Some read the Bible to learn and some read the Bible to hear from heaven." ~ Andrew Murray

God is speaking to us all the time. However, most of the time, we are not listening and even when we are, we are determined to hear what we want to hear rather than what the Lord has to say. I went around for some time telling people I could not hear God and how could I follow and obey if I did not know what He wanted of me... Yet, I believed the Holy Spirit was within me. How could I have the Spirit and not hear God? The truth of the matter is that we must believe we can hear before we will hear. Over the years, I have learned that as with most things with God, it requires us to believe before we will see any manifestation. The Word tells us it is impossible to please God without faith:

Hebrews 11:6 But without faith *it is* impossible to please *him*: for he that cometh to God must believe that he is, and *that* he is a rewarder of them that diligently seek him.

This is an area where the enemy really works hard to blind us to the truth. And, the truth is that we can hear God – if we believe. If we are His, then we can hear His voice!

John 10:27 My sheep hear my voice, and I know them, and they follow me:

Revelation 3:20 Behold, I stand at the door, and knock: if any man hear my voice, and open the door, I will come in to him, and will sup with him, and he with me.

This whole concept was critical to me. I had to learn to hear the voice of the Lord. I just had to - no matter what. I read everything I could find on "Hearing God", and it was all very proper and very detached. I had the notion that I must actually, physically hear the voice of God and if I did not or could not, I was lost. I had a good relationship with the Lord, but I knew more about Him than I actually knew Him. I was stuck in a very left-brained kind of loop where I could not hear, was convinced I could not hear and this became self-perpetuating.

Then, I ran across the web site of Mark Virkler, Communion with God Ministries, and his four keys to hearing God's voice in *4 Keys to Hearing God's Voice*. I think this literally saved me spiritually. The four keys to hearing God's voice are based on these verses of scripture:

Habakkuk 2:1 I will stand upon my watch, and set me upon the tower, and will watch to see what he will say unto me, and what I shall answer when I am reproved. 2 And the LORD answered me, and said, Write the vision, and make *it* plain upon tables, that he may run that readeth it.

The four keys to hearing God are:

1. God's voice in your heart often sounds like a flow of spontaneous thoughts.

2. Become still so you can sense God's flow of thoughts and emotions within.

3. As you pray, fix the eyes of your heart upon Jesus, seeing in the Spirit the dreams and visions of Almighty God.

4. Journaling, the writing out of your prayers and God's answers, brings great freedom in hearing God's voice.

The ability to hear God is critical and what I mentioned above is the bare minimum to get started. I fully and wholeheartedly recommend everyone obtain and study the Interactive Learning Experience, *4 Keys to Hearing God's Voice*, by Mark and Patti Virkler. You need to go through that marvelous book and study this area for yourself to make this a very real and growing part of your life.

Another thing we need to be wary of is allowing the clamor and noise of our circumstances to drown out the voice of the Spirit. And, in order to hear His Spirit, we have to practice. As we practice, we will get better and better at hearing Him. We must develop a greater expectation within us to hear His voice. God's willingness to speak is greater than our ability to hear! So, do not be afraid of hearing wrong. We must not doubt God – believing is always the better choice. The Lord will teach us to hear if we ask Him to and then expect Him to stand by His Word.

Mark 4:24 And he said unto them, Take heed what ye hear: with what measure ye mete, it shall be measured to you: and unto you that hear shall more be given.

We listen from our heart, not our head. We have an inbuilt receiver to hear God but it requires us to believe that we can hear and that God wants to speak to us. Will we make mistakes? Yes, but that is part of the learning process. Do not try to think it; rather feel God's voice within you. Listen in expectation. Still yourself down; be still and know that He is God.

Psalms 46:10 Be still, and know that I *am* God: I will be exalted among the heathen, I will be exalted in the earth.

Have you ever wanted a conversation with God? Not just talk to him but actually dialogue with him and hear his response to your questions? Below are some hands-on, practical steps that will help you to do just that. In John 10:4 and 10:27, Jesus said that His sheep know His voice. He did not mean that figuratively, but literally - His sheep know His voice. If you are a follower of Jesus, you have already recognized His voice at least once, and every person needs to practice listening to Him in order to correctly identify His voice at deeper and more personal levels.

Step One

Sit down with a notebook and a pen, still yourself down and ask God to speak to you. Then write down everything that comes to mind -- what you sense He might be telling you, even if it seems strange at the time. When you read over it later, you will be able to tell what was God and what was not (just as John 10:27 says), and you will be amazed at everything that was from God. Do not evaluate what you receive. Write it all down as you will evaluate it later. If you move from reception to analysis too quickly, it will block the flow.

Step Two

Be willing to hear things you were not expecting. If you do Step One and do not hear or sense anything, it may be that you are expecting to hear something in particular, and God wants to talk about something else. He might speak to you about something you have never thought of before. He is God, allow Him to drive.

Be open to anything He might say. It may take some time for you to learn to tell the difference between His voice and your own thoughts, but again, Jesus said that His sheep know His voice. He also said that if you ask for something good, He will not give you something evil in return:

Matthew 7:11 If ye then, being evil, know how to give good gifts unto your children, how much more shall your Father which is in heaven give good things to them that ask him?

If you are still having trouble, fix your eyes upon Jesus. Envision some story of the Gospels and then place yourself there in the story as a bystander. Place yourself in the scene. When I started doing this, I loved the story of the Samaritan woman at the well in John 4 and could visualize myself there as the exchange between Jesus and the Samaritan woman progressed.

Step Three

Do not despise small beginnings and do not try to analyze what comes to your mind, just write it down. You can analyze it later. Believe that God wants to speak to you and will speak to you simply because He loves you.

Realize that God can speak to us through anything: something that stands out to you as you are reading the newspaper or while writing your journal, talking with your child or sitting at your desk. God is more interested in you than you are in Him. Simply because that is true, you can expect to hear from Him.

Finally, here is a word of caution in all this. We all hear three voices – our own voice, the voice of God and the voice of the enemy. After some practice, you will get very good at discerning who was speaking at any given moment. But, here are some key things to remember:

- God does not accuse us – the enemy does. If you hear any word of accusation, you know it is from the enemy. He is called the accuser.
- God convicts and corrects us of sin because He loves us.
- Our voice tends to follow our emotions.
- God typically speaks His Word into us; i.e. verses from the Bible, as He has already spoken and recorded His word.
- Always measure what you hear against scripture. God will never contradict Himself. If what you heard does not line up with scripture, then it was from either you or the enemy.

Dear heavenly Father, thank you for every good thing that has ever come into my life. Thank you for Jesus, and for your Holy Spirit! Thank you for ears to hear and eyes to see! I thank you and praise you for teaching me to hear you clearly. Please help me to refine my hearing so I can always discern your voice from every other. And, Father please help me to always obey you in everything you bade me. In the name of Jesus I pray. Amen.

Loving Our Neighbor

"Intercessory prayer might be defined as loving our neighbor on our knees." ~ Charles Brent

Jesus was asked what the greatest commandment was and he replied:

Mark 12:29 And Jesus answered him, The first of all the commandments *is*, Hear, O Israel; The Lord our God is one Lord: 30 And thou shalt love the Lord thy God with all thy heart, and with all thy soul, and with all thy mind, and with all thy strength: this *is* the first commandment.

Then, He offered the second part of this:

Mark 12:31 And the second *is* like, *namely* this, Thou shalt love thy neighbour as thyself. There is none other commandment greater than these.

That is the whole thing right there. Love God, and love everyone else. Life is about love and about people. Love never, ever fails. In 1 Corinthians 13, replace the word charity (KJV) with love and you can see how important love is...

1 Corinthians 13:1 Though I speak with the tongues of men and of angels, and have not charity, I am become *as* sounding brass, or a tinkling cymbal. 2 And though I have *the gift of* prophecy, and understand all mysteries, and all knowledge; and though I have all faith, so that I could remove mountains, and have not charity, I am nothing. 3 And though I bestow all my goods to feed *the poor*, and though I give my body to be burned, and have not charity, it profiteth me nothing. 4 Charity suffereth long, *and* is kind; charity envieth not; charity vaunteth not itself, is not puffed up, 5 Doth not behave itself unseemly, seeketh not her own, is not easily provoked, thinketh no evil; 6 Rejoiceth not in iniquity, but rejoiceth in the truth; 7 Beareth all things, believeth all things,

hopeth all things, endureth all things. 8 Charity never faileth: but whether *there be* prophecies, they shall fail; whether *there be* tongues, they shall cease; whether *there be* knowledge, it shall vanish away. 9 For we know in part, and we prophesy in part. 10 But when that which is perfect is come, then that which is in part shall be done away. 11 When I was a child, I spake as a child, I understood as a child, I thought as a child: but when I became a man, I put away childish things. 12 For now we see through a glass, darkly; but then face to face: now I know in part; but then shall I know even as also I am known. 13 And now abideth faith, hope, charity, these three; but the greatest of these *is* charity.

We can also take verses 4 through 8 and replace the word charity with our loved ones name and make an awesome prayer of this scripture. I often do that for my spouse and other loved ones.

The hardest thing to learn about love is that we must love others, even those who seemingly do not deserve our love. Maybe, we should love them even more because they do not seem worthy of our love? We should bless those least deserving of our blessing. Surely, they need it more than those who already love God and are on the road to heaven. I feel we should bless and curse not, just as Jesus told us:

Romans 12:14 Bless them which persecute you: bless, and curse not.

If we only love and bless those who love and bless us, what have we gained? The wicked do that as well. We should also love those who use us despitefully. How about those who curse or persecute us?

Matthew 5:44 But I say unto you, Love your enemies, bless them that curse you, do good to them that hate you, and pray for them which despitefully use you, and persecute you; 45 That ye may be the children of your Father which is in heaven: for he maketh his sun to rise on the evil and on the good, and sendeth rain on the just and on the unjust. 46 For if ye love them which love you, what reward have ye? do not even the publicans the same? 47 And if ye salute your brethren only, what do ye more *than others*? do not even the publicans so? 48 Be ye therefore perfect, even as your Father which is in heaven is perfect.

Truly, loving our neighbor is a hard thing to ask of His people. Why would God want us to do that? Because, that is what He does. As stated above, He sends the rain on the just and the unjust and makes the sun to rise and shine on both the good and the evil.

When we feel God's love for someone in our heart, that is God in us wanting us to reach out and help that person through whatever it is they are facing. We are to be His hands, His feet, His heart to a lost and dying world. How can we do that without love?

I participated in some training by the Billy Graham Evangelistic Association, "Sharing Hope in Crisis" that is about their Rapid Response Team of Chaplains who respond to emergencies. One of the things that really struck me and has stayed with me to this day is the idea for every person in this world, no matter how good or how bad they may be, *that God knows their name.* Think about that when you see a person down on their luck, or just down – maybe for the final count due to some fault or affliction from the enemy. Maybe, it is their fault and they deserve what they are getting. But, what about grace; and, who made me judge and jury? Am I really getting what I deserve? No, no - I do not want what I deserve. I want grace!

We must learn to love others as much as we love ourselves. There is no other way to demonstrate Christ-likeness or the love of the Father for His creation. Our enemy hates every one of us simply because God does love us so much that He sent His only begotten son into the world:

John 3:16 For God so loved the world, that he gave his only begotten Son, that whosoever believes in him should not perish, but have everlasting life. 17 For God sent not his Son into the world to condemn the world; but that the world through him might be saved.

In summary, love never ever fails. We cannot do better than to love God and our neighbor as ourselves. Jesus told us that the one who does this fulfills all the requirements of the Torah.

Matthew 22:40 On these two commandments hang all the law and the prophets.

Oh Father God, please help me to love my neighbor as much as I love myself. Help me to remember that you know his name and that you love him as much as you love me. Help me to remember that he is my brother and we face a common enemy. Help me to be ready to help everyone I see who needs help and to show them Your love. In the priceless name of Jesus I pray. Amen.

Accountability partners

"What you do in your house is worth as much as if you did it up in heaven for our Lord God. We should accustom ourselves to think of our position and work as sacred and well-pleasing to God, not on account of the position and work, but on account of the word and faith from which the obedience and the work flow." ~ Martin Luther

It is a fact that sin, especially temptation and secret sin like darkness because they flourish there and if left there in the dark, they will indeed flourish and bloom. These sins typically are sins of the flesh. Pornography, homosexuality, adultery and other lustful sins (lust of the eyes and the lust of the flesh) easily fall into this category. Besetting sins are particularly difficult to get rid of, especially if we keep them hidden from others. What are besetting sins? Beset means:

1. To attack from all sides.
2. To trouble persistently; harass.
3. To hem in; surround: "the mountains which beset it round." (Nathaniel Hawthorne).

Hebrews 12:1 Wherefore seeing we also are compassed about with so great a cloud of witnesses, let us lay aside every weight, and the sin which doth so easily beset *us*, and let us run with patience the race that is set before us,

In the life of every person, there may be a "besetting" sin that can tower like a mountain between that person and God. This is "the sin which doth so easily beset us," and it differs according to the person. What is a besetting sin to one person may not trouble another at all. Sometimes this sin, or persistently assailing evil, is quite obvious to others, while in other cases it is hidden in the heart and known only to that person and God. In either case, it is perplexing and harassing, and, if allowed to linger and grow, it may end in tragic moral failure. Practically every believer wrestles with a habitually assaulting sin, even those whose service to Christ is of outstanding quality.

Romans 14:12 So then every one of us shall give account of himself to God.

Sin causes Christians to become craven cowards who live in humiliating and despondent defeat. They cannot stand with courage against sin because of the secret sin in their own lives. They often excuse the sins of other people because of the disobedience in their own hearts and they cannot preach victory because they live in defeat. Some of them once knew what it was like to live victoriously, living above the snake line. They experienced the power, the courage and the blessings that come to those who obey the Lord. Yet, today they are but a shadow of their old selves. Now they hang their heads in shame, unable to look the world in the eye, victimized by some sin that rules their lives. A besetting sin has robbed them of their spiritual vitality and one enemy after another is raised up against them.

We see it all the time. Some great Christian leader has an affair, or is caught cheating or gambling, or some small impropriety that seems to be nothing of concern to the masses will come to light. Or, a great deal of wickedness is exposed to the public in one way or another. Either way, God and our Lord Jesus are maligned, the enemies of Christianity snicker and point their fingers at us "Aha! Aha! You are no better than we are." The damage done to our faith, to the faith of those closest to the spectacle and certainly of the families involved is tremendous. It often completely shatters their lives. It will take years for all concerned to recover, if they ever do.

When a man or woman of God falls in this manner to some besetting sin, that person becomes a shell of what they were. They once stood in the pulpit as a powerful preacher of the Gospel and thousands were converted through their ministry. Later, they became an adulterer, left their spouse and ran off with another person. In just a few weeks, they lost everything. To see them shuffle about, beaten down and sad-eyed, is pitiful! They live in constant fear and spend sleepless nights thinking of what could have been. Their anxieties make them physically ill; they have heart pains, ulcers and hypertension. They have repented of their sin, but they cannot undo the past. God has forgiven them, but other people have not, and worst of all they cannot forgive themselves.

This person was overpowered by our enemies of guilt, fear and depression. They are a victim, defeated and humiliated by unseen forces that are set out to destroy them. Sin always allows the enemy access. Sin weakens our resistance; it turns warriors into weaklings. Lust starts in our mind, then sin comes, and sin allows the enemy in so he can destroy us.

The worst part about all this is that if the sin is not exposed, it will continue and become more deeply entrenched in that person's life until it completely consumes them. They repeat the sin and are ashamed of it. They repent and promise God it will never happen again. Something happens and they slip and sin again. The guilt is horrendous and unrelenting. It weighs on them like an anchor tied about their neck. They are sure everyone can see it and yet are determined that no one can ever know what they have been up to. Self-fulfilling and self-sustaining, the sin has now become a major part of them and it will take something akin to a bomb blast to separate them from it. This is the battle for our soul that many will have to face.

Proverbs 16:6 By mercy and truth iniquity is purged: and by the fear of the LORD *men* depart from evil.

How do we stand against such an onslaught? There is no easy formula that will work 100 percent of the time or guarantee success. But, there are some things we can do to level the playing field:

- Yearn for real holiness
- Hate whatever sin has hold of you

- Be utterly convinced that God loves you in spite of your sin
- Have faith that God will help you overcome this sin too
- Forgive everyone who has ever hurt you as we must forgive in order to be forgiven
- Find and nurture a relationship with an accountability partner

We have to honestly desire to be holy, because God is holy and He told us to be holy. We must hate whatever sin is attacking us. Not just dislike it, or merely to be ashamed of it – that will never suffice – we really have to hate it! We need to be completely and utterly convinced that God loves us in spite of our sin whatever it may be. He knew about it when He saved us and He knew we would have to go through this too. Since He knew about it and still loves us, He will help us to overcome that thing that is holding us. He will!

The next best thing to do after accomplishing all of the above is to find someone you really trust. Someone you can rely on to not divulge your secrets or think less of you because of them. For men, this will usually be another man and for women, it will usually be another woman. It does not have to be that way, but that is usually how it works out, and remember there is great danger in not selecting the right confessor!

James 5:16 Confess your faults one to another, and pray one for another, that you may be healed. The effectual fervent prayer of a righteous man avails much.

This person must become our confidant in that we share our darkest, most wicked secrets and sins with them and ask them to help us by praying for us and being an accountability partner so we will not succumb to that sin in the future. When we turn the lights on, on this type of sin it has no place to hide and it will be easier to deal with once it is out in the daylight. So, the best thing we can do is drag it into the light and expose it completely to at least one person we trust. This will remove the power it has over us. You see, as long as it was in the hall closet where no one looked, it was allowed to stay. It was locked away, safely hidden from anyone's eyes. We could visit it occasionally and no one would have to know about it. Once it is out of the closet, there is no place to hide now and that hook that was in us can be removed.

This is a process of sanctification and we will have to work our way through it. Do we appropriate sanctification? Or is it a matter of killing something that is in us that should not be there? Freedom still requires responsibility. We want to be free – free from sin, evil and temptation. As long as we harbor some secret thing, or some secret sin we can never be free.

Oh Mighty God, please help me to become real with myself and others. Help me overcome all the devices of the enemy by finding and nurturing a relationship with someone who can hear my full confession without judging me. Help me Father by giving me courage and strength in face of glaring evil and help me to stand and face it down with your help. In the matchless name of Jesus I pray. Amen.

Keys to Success

"You have within you now all the elements that are necessary to make you all that the Father dreamed that you would be in Christ. "
~ E. W. Kenyon

Romans 8:37 Nay, in all these things we are more than conquerors through him that loved us.

Micah 6:8 He hath shewed thee, O man, what is good; and what doth the LORD require of thee, but to do justly, and to love mercy, and to walk humbly with thy God?

Psalms 139:23-24 Search me, O God, and know my heart: try me, and know my thoughts: 24 And see if there be any wicked way in me, and lead me in the way everlasting.

The key to success in most things in life stem from a passion for what you believe in, a clear vision of where you are going and the drive to stick to whatever it is you are passionate about. If it is not important enough for you to sacrifice your time, efforts and money, it will not be important to anyone else either. This Christian life is not easy, but it is achievable and attainable for everyone who spends the effort to live this way.

I have found there are several keys that enhance our ability to stay on course no matter how hard the road may seem, and no matter how fierce the opposition we face is to this warrior lifestyle. In Proverbs, Solomon tells us to set our face like flint, neither turning to the left nor to the right, but holding dead on, straight on for the things of God:

Proverbs 4:25 Let thine eyes look right on, and let thine eyelids look straight before thee. 26 Ponder the path of thy feet, and let all thy ways be established. 27 Turn not to the right hand nor to the left: remove thy foot from evil.

We have to make up our own minds about a few things and then stick to our guns so to speak. We cannot be fluctuating or wavering about how we live this Christian life. The bible also talks about an unstable man:

James 1:8 A double minded man *is* unstable in all his ways.

If we waver, and do not get up each day determined to live as Jesus would have us to live, renew our dedication to serve Him fully and then fight the good fight of faith, we will fall back into our sinful ways. The pressures against us are just too strong.

Here are some keys I found that help me stay the course:

Accepted

"Do not let your happiness depend on something you may lose... only (upon) the Beloved who will never pass away." ~ C.S. Lewis

Ephesians 1:6 To the praise of the glory of his grace, wherein he hath made us accepted in the beloved.

Deuteronomy 33:12 And of Benjamin he said, The beloved of the LORD shall dwell in safety by him; and the LORD shall cover him all the day long, and he shall dwell between his shoulders.

The image I get from the last verse is a father bearing his children upon his shoulders. What a wonderful portrait of how God accepts us! He would carry us upon His shoulders! This is the only verse in all scripture that contains the phrase "the beloved of the Lord." It helps me think of God as Abba, daddy. After all throwing your child up on your shoulder so they can see better, or just hitch a ride or just to have them close is such a marvelous expression of love, it sounds just like something God would do.

The first time I heard *The Father's Love Letter*,[1] it was done by Leif Hetland who began the session by proclaiming he loved to climb up into Abba's, his Daddy's, lap and just rest there. He was speaking about God! This too changed my life as my previous notions of God were all about Him being high and lifted up, far away from anyone like me. I knew God was big, wonderful and awesome but I did not know He actually loved me personally. I had always pictured Him as very austere and aloof, set apart from anything human because we were so corrupt. I had never considered that what the bible said about His love was real. Oh, I had heard it and professed to believe it, but I truly did not believe that God could really love a creature like me.

I know a lot of people who still feel that way, and it is a real shame because if they only knew how much God really does love them, they could overcome so many of the obstacles in their lives. As a spiritual warrior, anointed by God to serve Him, we must come to terms with this whole idea. We are loved more than we can imagine. More than we have ever been loved by any other person in this world. We are part of the beloved. The beloved of Jesus Christ and we are loved as much as the beloved disciple was loved by our Lord.

John 15:15 Henceforth I call you not servants; for the servant knoweth not what his lord doeth: but I have called you friends; for all things that I have heard of my Father I have made known unto you.

We must accept the fact that we are friends of God. There has been much debate about who the beloved disciple was. Was it John the son of Zebedee, Lazarus, Mary Magdalene or some other candidate? I respectfully submit that I think the beloved disciple is us, you and I; the little anointed ones of God who have surrendered all to follow hard after Jesus.

John 6:51 I am the living bread which came down from heaven: if any man eat of this bread, he shall live for ever: and the bread that I will give is my flesh, which I will give for the life of the world.

John 6:57 As the living Father hath sent me, and I live by the Father: so he that eateth me, even he shall live by me. 58 This is that bread which came down from heaven: not as your fathers did eat manna, and are dead: he that eateth of this bread shall live for ever.

John 11:25 Jesus said unto her, I am the resurrection, and the life: he that believeth in me, though he were dead, yet shall he live:

We have eaten the bread of life, and received Jesus as our Lord and Master. We have dedicated everything about our lives to Jesus. We are striving to learn and become all he wants us to learn and become. We are being changed from glory to glory. We are in the beloved and the beloved is in us!

John 17:9 I pray for them: I pray not for the world, but for them which thou hast given me; for they are thine. 10 And all mine are thine, and thine are mine; and I am glorified in them.

John 17:21 That they all may be one; as thou, Father, art in me, and I in thee, that they also may be one in us: that the world may believe that thou hast sent me. 22 And the glory which thou gavest me I have given them; that they may be one, even as we are one: 23 I in them, and thou in me, that they may be made perfect in one; and that the world may know that thou hast sent me, and hast loved them, as thou hast loved me.

We are accepted and loved by Father God! He sees us as we will be, perfected in heaven. We are seated in heavenly places in Christ Jesus. Believe it and receive it! Praise God for His loving kindness!

Ephesians 2:6 And hath raised us up together, and made us sit together in heavenly places in Christ Jesus:

We need to know God's forgiveness as more than a theological idea; that there is nothing that God has not forgiven us, means that we can unconditionally believe that He really loves us – every single bit of us. This acceptance is totally life transforming!

Commitment

"The ultimate measure of a man is not where he stands in moments of comfort and convenience, but where he stands at times of challenge and controversy." ~ Martin Luther King Jr.

Early in my Christian walk, I spent a period of over a year getting up every day and telling myself that I was dead to sin, evil and temptation and alive to the Spirit of life in Christ Jesus.

Romans 8:2 For the law of the Spirit of life in Christ Jesus hath made me free from the law of sin and death.

You see, it is the Spirit of life in Christ Jesus that does the work of setting us free. It has released us from the spirit of death, of sin, evil and temptation. But, we have to walk it out. We have to separate ourselves wholly and outright from this world and the lust and pride it lures us with. We must be willing to cut our arm off to save our life!

1 John 2:16 For all that is in the world, the lust of the flesh, and the lust of the eyes, and the pride of life, is not of the Father, but is of the world.

During the winter of 1913, John G. Lake presented a sermon to the Church of England entitled, "Triune Salvation."[2] In this study, he reveals the important significance of our complete redemption on all three levels of life: the complete redemption of our spirit, perfect deliverance of our soul (mind) and complete freedom of our body.

1 Thessalonians 5:23 And the very God of peace sanctify you wholly; and I pray God your whole spirit and soul and body be preserved blameless unto the coming of our Lord Jesus Christ.

He taught that the average Christian ceased in their search for God at the atonement of their spirit. He believed it is vitally important that the believer allows the Holy Spirit to also sanctify both the soul and the body. This is so a person can truly become the habitation of God.

1 Corinthians 2:16 For who hath known the mind of the Lord, that he may instruct him? But we have the mind of Christ.

The sanctification of the soul literally involves the impartation of the mind of Christ. John Wesley defined sanctification as "possessing the mind of Christ and all the mind of Christ." This level of consecration is essential for our thoughts to be perfectly in tune with the Lord's thoughts and our ways to be consistent with His ways.

Complete triune salvation also involves the separation of the believer from all that defiles him, recognizing our body is the temple of the Holy Spirit and should be consecrated accordingly.

Romans 8:11 But if the Spirit of him that raised up Jesus from the dead dwell in you, he that raised up Christ from the dead shall also quicken your mortal bodies by his Spirit that dwelleth in you.

The Lord's imparted life granted through the indwelling presence of the Holy Spirit provides both divine health and freedom from the lusts of the flesh, and the lusts of the eyes. John Lake taught that the genuine Christian is a separated person. Separated wholly and completely to God in every facet of life; body, soul and spirit are committed forever to the Lord. This absolute abandonment to God is the secret to the successful Christian life and is essential to become the habitation of God.

Without holiness the complete purpose of the Church cannot be fulfilled. Holiness and sanctification are often used interchangeably in Scripture. A holy and sanctified condition can only happen when we overcome our flesh nature. Once the depravity and depths of our soul are uncovered we can then call upon God's grace to separate us from all that is of this world. It takes total separation from everything that is ungodly to purge our spirit, soul and body from every evil tendency and influence.

The indwelling presence of the Holy Spirit makes the believer a master over every power of darkness that is in the world. We are to be God's representatives in this world. The presence of the Holy Spirit is to be as powerful in our lives as He was in the life of Jesus. Therefore, fear of evil spirits and demonic opposition is totally out of the question. Not because of our merits but because of the Lord's dominion and victory.

Colossians 1:27 To whom God would make known what is the riches of the glory of this mystery among the Gentiles; which is Christ in you, the hope of glory:

John G. Lake believed the secret to this Christian life is not in doing but in being. It is in being the possessor of the divine nature of Jesus Christ and His awesome and empowering presence. We are to reflect Christ's character and message in the demonstration of the Spirit and power. It is by becoming one with the Father that we know peace in the midst of storms. It is through the Lord's abiding presence; we find the secret place of the most high and abide under the shadow of the Almighty.

Psalms 91:1 He that dwelleth in the secret place of the most High shall abide under the shadow of the Almighty.

Consistency

"It is time to quit playing church and start being the church." ~ Keith Green

Consistency requires discipline and tenacity in order to be effective. I read once where Kenneth Copeland told his people that God told him the key to living a Christian life was consistency. Getting up each day, spending time with God, reading His Word, praying and trying to live right; these are the things that bring success.

Philippians 1:27 Only let your conversation be as it becometh the gospel of Christ: that whether I come and see you, or else be absent, I may hear of your affairs, that ye stand fast in one spirit, with one mind striving together for the faith of the gospel;

If you fall, or sin and think you are never going to make it; do not be disappointed. We have all felt that way. What do you do? Confess your sin to the Father, repent and pick yourself up again and start again. Make up your mind that nothing, NO THING will ever be able to stop you from fully pursuing God and trying to live in His light. That is the key. Be tenacious, never give up or give in. just start over again to do the things you know to do. God is faithful and He will help you.

Obedience

"The golden rule for understanding in spiritual matters is not intellect, but obedience." ~ Oswald Chambers

Obedience is a tough trait for many of us. Most of us seem to specialize in rebellion. Rebelling against authority or authority figures in particular seem to go hand in hand with growing up. I can still see my back getting stiff when I hear someone say "obey me." And, I see the same thing in my own children. I am not really sure why we (people in general) are so hard headed but I know the bible talked about the Israelites being stiff necked:

Deuteronomy 31:27 For I know thy rebellion, and thy stiff neck: behold, while I am yet alive with you this day, ye have been rebellious against the LORD; and how much more after my death?

Jeremiah 17:23 But they obeyed not, neither inclined their ear, but made their neck stiff, that they might not hear, nor receive instruction.

If you think about it, you can make your neck stiff right now. Try it. It is not a pleasant thing to do and I can feel the rebellion rise up in me when I do it. The worst part of rebellion is that the crime of rebellion is like unto witchcraft:

1 Samuel 15:16 Then Samuel said unto Saul, Stay, and I will tell thee what the LORD hath said to me this night. And he said unto him, Say on. 17 And Samuel said, When thou *wast* little in thine own sight, *wast* thou not *made* the head of the tribes of Israel, and the LORD anointed thee king over Israel? 18 And the LORD sent thee on a journey, and said, Go and utterly destroy the sinners the Amalekites, and fight against them until they be consumed. 19 Wherefore then didst thou not obey the voice of the LORD, but didst fly upon the spoil, and didst evil in the sight of the LORD? 20 And Saul said unto Samuel, Yea, I have obeyed the voice of the LORD, and have gone the way which the LORD sent me, and have

brought Agag the king of Amalek, and have utterly destroyed the Amalekites. 21 But the people took of the spoil, sheep and oxen, the chief of the things which should have been utterly destroyed, to sacrifice unto the LORD thy God in Gilgal. 22 And Samuel said, Hath the LORD *as great* delight in burnt offerings and sacrifices, as in obeying the voice of the LORD? Behold, to obey *is* better than sacrifice, *and* to hearken than the fat of rams. 23 For rebellion *is as* the sin of witchcraft, and stubbornness *is as* iniquity and idolatry. Because thou hast rejected the word of the LORD, he hath also rejected thee from *being* king.

Saul was anointed as the first king over Israel, yet he lost it all when he refused to obey God. He tried to make up for it by making burnt offerings with the things they took as spoil. But, you see partial or slow obedience is really disobedience. There is no way around that. When we know what God wants us to do, we should comply and obey immediately; anything less than that is disobedience.

Proverbs 17:11 An evil *man* seeketh only rebellion: therefore a cruel messenger shall be sent against him.

Romans 6:16 Know ye not, that to whom ye yield yourselves servants to obey, his servants ye are to whom ye obey; whether of sin unto death, or of obedience unto righteousness?

Disobedience is always met with punishment.

Ephesians 5:6 Let no man deceive you with vain words: for because of these things cometh the wrath of God upon the children of disobedience.

Colossians 3:6 For which things' sake the wrath of God cometh on the children of disobedience:

In order to get back into the good grace of God, where we were in Him, we must obey Him. Some people have told me that God used to speak to them all the time, but now He does not speak to them at all. When I inquire further, I discover that they did not obey the voice of the Lord the last time he issued a decree to them. If you sense silence from heaven, check to ensure you obeyed the last thing God spoke to you. He usually will not issue any more commands to us until the last one He issued has been complied with.

Jeremiah 26:13 Therefore now amend your ways and your doings, and obey the voice of the LORD your God; and the LORD will repent him of the evil that he hath pronounced against you.

Remember, obedience is better than sacrifice! If God is sovereign and Lord of our lives, we must obey Him quickly and completely.

No Compromise

"A little lie is like a little pregnancy, it does not take long before everyone knows." ~ C. S. Lewis

Compromising with sin, with temptation or with the culture of death is a sure way to stop all spiritual growth and definitely puts us in harm's way. The world will tell you not to worry about it as everyone else is thinking about doing it or doing it. Whatever it is does not really matter. We know our Lord and we know His ways and what He wants from us. And, it is infinitely better than anything this world has to offer. We are to stand above all sin and all evil:

Romans 12:9 Let love be without hypocrisy. Abhor that which is evil; cleave to that which is good.

James 3:17 But the wisdom that is from above is first pure, then peaceable, gentle, and easy to be intreated, full of mercy and good fruits, without partiality, and without hypocrisy.

To walk in hypocrisy, which is compromise with the enemy will bring evil into our lives as we live the lie and try to persuade others that we are righteous.

1 Timothy 4:2 Speaking lies in hypocrisy; having their conscience seared with a hot iron;

Having our conscience seared with a hot iron is the same as cauterizing a wound, specifically a wound of the mind and of our soul. Once our conscience is seared, it becomes harder and harder to respond properly to the unction of the Holy Spirit. Compromise can be likened to the spectacle of putting a frog into a pot of cool water and turning the heat up very slowly. Eventually, the frog is cooked to death but he never sensed it until perhaps it was too late to do anything about it.

The church is not supposed to look like the rest of the world. We are to be set apart, holy for the Lord. I once asked the Lord why people were so caught up in tattoos and piercings. The answer I received surprised me at first, but makes complete sense to me now. We are made in the image of God. The enemy hates us because we look like God and he wants us to mar and disfigure ourselves because to him, it is a marring and disfiguring of God Almighty too.

Leviticus 19:28 Ye shall not make any cuttings in your flesh for the dead, nor print any marks upon you: I am the LORD.

I have had many people tell me they get tattoos to honor God. Disobedience does not honor God. Our God is a God of love and mercy. He does not want us to cut, pierce and mark ourselves in order to please Him. I know this is not something many people want to hear, but the truth is still the truth. Having already done these things will not separate us from God's love, but we could have avoided all the pain and potential for serious infection, as well as the mess and cost of these alterations.

Even where we work or go to school or just in our neighborhood, people may reject or argue with the words we say. But they will never refute or forget our acts of love. Do not let petty sins and spiritual compromises cast a shadow over our example. We can live above reproach and let the light of Jesus shine brightly through us.

Bless Others

"Being loved is life's second greatest blessing; loving is the greatest." ~ Jack Hyles

Become one who blesses other men - we can increase the anointing upon our lives by becoming a person who blesses other men. The process of blessing others increases the anointing upon our own lives. Blessing means to empower. It is God's empowerment, the same power that created the universe. As the Word states it, the lesser is blessed of the better:

Hebrews 7:7 And without all contradiction the less is blessed of the better.

God made man in His own image and then blessed him, and empowered him to accomplish all He made him for:

Genesis 1:28 And God blessed them, and God said unto them, Be fruitful, and multiply, and replenish the earth, and subdue it: and have dominion over the fish of the sea, and over the fowl of the air, and over every living thing that moveth upon the earth.

Man sinned and fell, and men in general became very wicked. In fact, people became so wicked that God was forced to destroy the earth and everything in it using water. But, there was one family who did not follow after the world, so God used them to start over and He blessed them:

Genesis 9:1 And God blessed Noah and his sons, and said unto them, Be fruitful, and multiply, and replenish the earth.

We have the opportunity to bless those we encounter in this life. I bless my children every night as I put them to bed. I bless other people's children whenever I sense God moving in that direction. I bless nearly everyone I communicate with. I am not sure exactly when all this started, but I feel compelled to bless other people. Maybe, it is because we need it so much. Paul's instructions to the church in Romans 12 contain clear instructions about this:

Romans 12:14 Bless them which persecute you: bless, and curse not.

We have neighbors that have always kept to themselves, very private people who seemed to have one controversy or fight with other neighbors going on at all times. Many times it was over a dog, or some boundary infraction that created an offense between them. I was talking to another one of my neighbors one day and they were complaining about this couple, and I heard myself say that there must be something wrong in their lives for there to be so much turmoil and that someone should pray for them.

Well, God convicted me right there – I had not been praying for them either. So, I started praying for them, and my other neighbors. When I drove by their home, I would bless them in the name of Jesus. My daughter and I started blessing them every time we drove by. Within two weeks, these folks started coming outside, working in the yard, waving and smiling at their neighbors. In the ten plus years I had known them, they never did that! What changed? The only thing different I knew of was that we were now blessing them.

Blessing works! God is faithful and good, every day! I have read many times now where scientists are baffled why one set of plants will outgrow and outperform another set of plants with identical environmental and physical traits. They had the same source for the seed, same water, same light and same fertilizer. What is the difference? One set was blessed daily – spoken over with kind soothing words or with soft soothing music being played while the other set was either deprived of that, or got the opposite. Hard, harsh words or hard rock music was played or spoken over that set of plants. The results are astounding scientists and others who do not know our Lord. But, this should not be a surprise to us.

The bible is full of details why the blessing works and why curses do the opposite. All we have to do is try the same thing in our lives. If we apply what the bible says, we can change the atmosphere around us, our neighborhoods, our towns and cities and even our countries. Bless and curse not!

I have seen it over and over again now. Take a young man who has never been told God loves him, and who has never had strong words of encouragement spoken over him or into his life, and do just that. Tell him that God loves him, and that he can be good, faithful and fruitful, and that he has a hope and an expected end. Bless him in the name of Jesus. Then, watch what God will do for and in that man.

I bless people on the road. When traffic is really bad, or I feel the unction of the Lord, I bless the people in the cars and all their occupants in the name of Jesus. It is a proven fact that if we bless the intersections where the worst accidents occur, there will not be as many accidents and their severity will be lesser. The same thing happens in bad neighborhoods. Take a team and walk and pray and bless that neighborhood for a period of time. Then, watch as the crime rate goes down and the whole atmosphere in that neighborhood changes to something more positive.

You see, our words have power. God created everything with words. He said let there be light and there was light. We have the power of life and death in our mouth, and we need to learn to use it for life:

Proverbs 18:21 Death and life are in the power of the tongue: and they that love it shall eat the fruit thereof.

Watch what you say, and purposefully bless other people you encounter. Something great will happen in your life and in those around you! Remember, the one who needs the blessing the most is probably the one who deserves it the least.

Let me speak into your life right now:

> The LORD will bless you, and He will keep you:

The LORD will make his face shine upon you, and He will be gracious unto you:

The LORD will lift up his countenance upon you, and He will give you Shalom.   Numbers 6:24-26

Most people know shalom means peace but it also means completeness, wholeness, health, peace, welfare, safety, soundness, tranquility, prosperity, perfectness, fullness, rest, harmony, the absence of agitation or discord. Shalom comes from the root verb shalom meaning to be complete, perfect and full.

In other words, the word shalom is a mighty blessing! So, be blessed in the matchless name of Jesus!

Father, in the name of Jesus, I claim Your blessing today. I rejoice in Your love for me and my family and Your desire to bless our lives. I thank You for strong faith and a heart that is fixed toward You. I believe the blessings of Heaven are multiplied in my life, my family, my work and my church. Amen

Faith and Hope

"There is something about believing God that will cause Him to pass over a million people to get to you because of your faith." ~ Smith Wigglesworth

Hebrews 11:1 Now faith is the substance of things hoped for, the evidence of things not seen.

We need faith and hope to face the difficulties we will face and to stand when everything else in this world seems to be against us. How do we build our faith?

1. We listen and obey God. If God tells us to do something, or not to do something, we should obey instantly. If He is in it, it is all good and He will see that it is accomplished. If He is not in it, we do not want any part of it as it will be dependent on our strength and wits only, which is a very precarious place to be.

2. Journal – record your prayers and the answers to your prayers, and all communication from God.

3. Get up every day and recite the affirmation scriptures that speak to your heart.

All this will build your faith. We should never let the enemy talk us out of obeying God, or into doing something against God's express Word. If we do, we are sure to fail. We need to anticipate what God is going to do to support us, to defend and protect us and to help us in every situation. Since we have God, we have hope. We know he is a strong tower.

Psalms 61:3 For thou hast been a shelter for me, *and* a strong tower from the enemy.

Proverbs 18:10 The name of the LORD *is* a strong tower: the righteous runneth into it, and is safe.

Where is the best place to be? Right, smack dab in the center of God's will for our lives. If we reside there, we will have peace, faith and hope in abundance because God cannot fail, He cannot fail us and He cannot make a mistake. The exact center verse of the Holy Bible seems like it would be the center of God's will for us:

Psalms 118:8 It is better to trust in the LORD than to put confidence in man.

Amazing, huh? Do you think maybe God planned it that way? Of course He did! In Hebrew, there is no word for coincidence!

Jeremiah 17:7 Blessed *is* the man that trusteth in the LORD, and whose hope the LORD is.

I once had the voice of God tell me "I do not make mistakes." That got my attention right away. I remember I was whining about something I had done and telling God He made a mistake when He made me. He answered immediately and I heard His audible voice, right behind my ear.

It startled me so bad I was looking around trying to find Him. But, it really lifted me out of a very dark place I was working my way into. You see, God is always faithful. He is always at our right hand, and He will never fail us or leave us. What an awesome God He is! We can rely on Him completely!

Hebrews 6:17-19 Wherein God, willing more abundantly to shew unto the heirs of promise the immutability of his counsel, confirmed it by an oath: 18 That by two immutable things, in which it was impossible for God to lie, we might have a strong consolation, who have fled for refuge to lay hold upon the hope set before us: 19 Which hope we have as an anchor of the soul, both sure and stedfast, and which entereth into that within the veil;

Favor of the Most High

"Grace is the free, undeserved goodness and favor of God to mankind." ~ Matthew Henry

Proverbs 22:1 A good name is rather to be chosen than great riches, and loving favour rather than silver and gold.

Psalms 5:12 For thou, LORD, wilt bless the righteous; with favour wilt thou compass him as with a shield.

So, what is favor? In the Webster dictionary the definition of favor includes: friendly or kind regard; good will; approval; liking; unfair partiality; favoritism; attractiveness; to be partial to; prefer; to help; assist; to do a kindness for; endorsing. To be favored means: regarded or treated with favor; provided with advantages; especially privileged.

People often will ask me "how are you doing?" Or, "how are you?" I nearly always answer, "I am blessed and walk in the favor of the Most High." I am not bragging or being boastful in any way, merely stating a fact. I do walk in the awesome and delightful favor of God. You see, God likes me. I know we are supposed to believe God loves us, but can He really like a fallen creature like man? You bet He does!

You must understand God sees us as we will be, not as we are. He sees His completed work in us! Imagine that for a moment. The Word tells us God knew the end before He began the work. Our Father is not constrained by time as we are. He can come and go, in and out of time as He pleases. He can enter any time frame and do whatever He pleases and exit that time and enter again at another point, at will. So, our Father sees us as we will be someday – perfect and full of His glory, made in the express image of His son Jesus. Glory! Hallelujah! It is shouting time!

1 John 3:22 And whatsoever we ask, we receive of him, because

we keep his commandments, and do those things that are pleasing in his sight.

If God sees us perfected, why do we insist on dragging out the dead cat to show everyone? Our entire life span on earth is nothing more a single drop of water in the wide Pacific Ocean when compared to eternity. When we were born again, we began a journey that will last forever. The Word tells us God knew us before He set the foundations of the world. In my heart, I know that God knew who would love Him this very day before He created any physical thing.

That is why we can have our petitions and needs met so completely. We may not see it for a while in our time line, but when we ask in Jesus' name, and in accordance with the Father's will, we will receive what we ask for! I believe our prayers are answered immediately, and we need to be patient enough for God's favor and time to align, and then we will see the manifestation.

Job 10:12 Thou hast granted me life and favour, and thy visitation hath preserved my spirit.

Proverbs 12:2 A good man obtaineth favour of the LORD: but a man of wicked devices will he condemn.

Luke 2:52 And Jesus increased in wisdom and stature, and in favour with God and man.

Watch Your Vows

"If God takes our idle words seriously, how much more seriously does He take those words spoken with forethought? And if He takes our normal statements seriously, how much more seriously does He take our promises, especially when those promises are raised to the level of the formal vow?" ~ R.C. Sproul

There is a story in the book of Judges that breaks my heart every time I read it. It is the story of Jephthah, a judge of Israel who made a foolish vow that cost him his only daughter. As warriors, we need to watch and guard our mouths that no evil comes forth from us. Words we speak take on a life of their own and we can see what we speak into others come to pass in their lives. I dare say, there is no more powerful force emanating from a man than his voice.

Deuteronomy 30:19 I call heaven and earth to record this day against you, that I have set before you life and death, blessing and cursing: therefore choose life, that both thou and thy seed may live:

Jephthah did not have to utter this vow. The spirit of the Lord had already come upon him, and the Lord would never want us to make a vow like this. In fact, Jesus tells us let our yes be yes and our no be no and that anything other than that is evil.

Matthew 5:37 But let your communication be, Yea, yea; Nay, nay: for whatsoever is more than these cometh of evil.

I am not sure why Jephthah made such a devastating vow. Perhaps, he thought he had to bargain with the Lord. But, that is completely unreasonable. God is always good and wants to bless us. Maybe he did it to impress those around him. He did have a persecution complex after he had been cast out early in his life. Whatever the reason was, here was his vow:

Judges 11:29-31 Then the Spirit of the LORD came upon Jephthah,

The Warrior Anointing, destiny awaits

and he passed over Gilead, and Manasseh, and passed over Mizpeh of Gilead, and from Mizpeh of Gilead he passed over unto the children of Ammon. 30 And Jephthah vowed a vow unto the LORD, and said, If thou shalt without fail deliver the children of Ammon into mine hands, 31 Then it shall be, that whatsoever cometh forth of the doors of my house to meet me, when I return in peace from the children of Ammon, shall surely be the LORD'S, and I will offer it up for a burnt offering.

He vowed to offer up as a burnt sacrifice whatever came forth from his own home and greeted him upon his return. This is a fatal mistake. It is fatal to the one who greets him and I am sure he never completely recovered from the loss he incurred due to his own rash statement.

Judges 11:34-40 And Jephthah came to Mizpeh unto his house, and, behold, his daughter came out to meet him with timbrels and with dances: and she was his only child; beside her he had neither son nor daughter. 35 And it came to pass, when he saw her, that he rent his clothes, and said, Alas, my daughter! thou hast brought me very low, and thou art one of them that trouble me: for I have opened my mouth unto the LORD, and I cannot go back. 36 And she said unto him, My father, if thou hast opened thy mouth unto the LORD, do to me according to that which hath proceeded out of thy mouth; forasmuch as the LORD hath taken vengeance for thee of thine enemies, even of the children of Ammon. 37 And she said unto her father, Let this thing be done for me: let me alone two months, that I may go up and down upon the mountains, and bewail my virginity, I and my fellows. 38 And he said, Go. And he sent her away for two months: and she went with her companions, and bewailed her virginity upon the mountains. 39 And it came to pass at the end of two months, that she returned unto her father, who did with her according to his vow which he had vowed: and she knew no man. And it was a custom in Israel, 40 That the daughters of Israel went yearly to lament the daughter of Jephthah the Gileadite four days in a year.

What a devastating vow this turned out to be. But, both Jephthah and his daughter honored his vow before God. And, we must honor our vows or we are nothing. Our word should be our bond. If you cannot believe what I say, you will never trust me in anything. I grew up this way. A man's word was his bond. You could take some men's word to the bank and they would honor that word simply because they knew the man who uttered it.

Numbers 30:2 If a man vow a vow unto the LORD, or swear an oath to bind his soul with a bond; he shall not break his word, he shall do according to all that proceedeth out of his mouth.

So, be very careful what you vow!

Be a Voice, not an Echo

"Do not talk to others about your problem, speak to the problem about your God!" ~ Carl-Gustaf Severin

During the last week of October, 2011, a story[3] broke about a scandal involving a former member of the coaching staff of Penn State University. A man who was respected and revered by so many now stands accused of molesting ten or more boys. He used his position as a coach to get near them, to stay near them and to exploit them – sexually. Even worse, it appears as though many other coaches and people in respected and well placed positions within the university were aware of the problem, at least to one degree or another, and yet did nothing to protect the innocent young men who were this predator's prey.

These bystanders at Penn State had nine years to report the alleged sins of the former coach but did nothing. Why didn't they report the suspected abuse? Could it have been lust for money, wealth, power, prestige or all of the above? So many lives damaged and the reputation of the school and faculty forever impinged. By looking the other way, they now find themselves covered in shame, for the Bible promises,

Numbers 32:23 But if ye will not do so, behold, ye have sinned against the LORD: and be sure your sin will find you out.

Are these actions wrong because there is moral outrage against them? Or are they wrong because these actions are first and foremost horrible sins committed against God Himself? The stories of the evil at Penn State did not mention God or His holiness at all. Our society believes that we ourselves are the source for knowing what is right from what is wrong. We assume we are accountable only to ourselves. There has not been one person speak of the sin of the people that are involved. Yet, they did sin against God.

Too many other sins are callously overlooked. For example, where are the outcries against the millions of children who have been robbed of life in their mother's wombs? Where are the outcries against the pressure exerted on young women and men by many educators and by the cultural elites to engage in sex outside of marriage, or homosexual activity?

Proverbs 24:11-12 If thou forbear to deliver them that are drawn unto death, and those that are ready to be slain; 12 If thou sayest, Behold, we knew it not; doth not he that pondereth the heart consider it? and he that keepeth thy soul, doth not he know it? and shall not he render to every man according to his works?

We see people all around us who are in trouble, in way over their heads in situations where they cannot seem to find their way out. They are headed for certain destruction and yet we remain silent. We allow political correctness and polite society to dictate what we will allow. We refrain from getting involved because it is too messy, or will take too much time, or we are afraid whatever they have or whatever they were doing might rub off onto us!

Time and time again we see similar stories surface where some respected leader either from secular society or even the faith based camp strays from the path of integrity, honor and morality into a quagmire of lust and sin. It is revolting and sickening.

We need to live above reproach and become true spiritual warriors who will not compromise with sin, evil or temptation. If something is wrong, or evil, then it is wrong. We cannot sugar coat or gloss over known sin as though "boys will be boys" or some other inane simile as though it is Ok because others are doing it. If it is wrong, do not do it! If you know about it, shout it to the authorities. We must embarrass sin and expose it to the light, or it will come back on us and embarrass us.

Taking this whole notion one step further, people have a terrible tendency to kill one another off through genocide[4]:

China, Mao Ze-Dong	49 to to 78 Million
Russia, Joseph Stalin	23 Million
Germany, Adolf Hitler	12 Million
Belgium, Leopold II	8 Million
Japan, Hideki Tojo	5 Million
Cambodia, Pol Pot	1.7 Million
North Korea, Kim Sung	1.6 Million
Turkey, Armenians	300,000 - 1.5 Million
Rwanda, Abatutsi & Abahutu	.5 to 1 Million
Bosnia	200,000 +
Sudan	200,000 to 400,000

Why is there so much death and destruction? Could it be because the enemy of our soul is using people to hurt, maim and kill other people? It is hard to wrap our minds around why one people would go to such lengths to exterminate another people. Yet, it happened all through history and is still happening today! When one life is deemed of lesser value than another, then it is not so hard to end that inferior life.

Just the other day, I heard a story[5] where brain surgeons here in America were told that patients over 70 years of age will not be offered the most expensive surgical options due to their age. These "units," (they are now referred to as units instead of people) were much too old for that. The Japanese at Camp 731[6] during WWII called people "maruta," meaning "logs of wood." The Nazi's also referred to people as units. It is sad to see that we still refer to people as some type of thing or anything other than people.

This is often done purportedly in the best interests of the public or some other noble cause. Sometimes, it is pure revenge; most often though, it is simply economics. As Christians, we are supposed to love everyone, even our enemies. If we will not come up higher and live a life of integrity and virtue, we will be doomed to follow in the same footsteps as earlier generations.

We can make a difference just by being real and always standing for truth, honor and integrity no matter what challenges us. There are a great many people who understand the times we are living in but are not sure how they should respond or whether or not they should take a risk at all. Our lives mean so much more than anything this world has to offer. We must be real, be fully engaged as our brother's keeper, and always try to do the right thing in every situation.

We need to stop being quiet, stop allowing evil to have it's way and become what we are called to be – men and women of valor. We need to be ready to rise up and defend the defenseless, the orphaned, the destitute and the disenfranchised.

We know what the right thing is in every problem or situation we face. Sometimes, we allow ourselves to become confused because the right way may cost us more money, more time or more effort. But, we know. We really do know and we must listen to the Holy Spirit and follow His guidance if we want to make a difference in the lives of those we love and care about, and in the lives of so many other people.

There are many times I have embarrassed my older children because I would not budge on some issue. I really was not trying to aggravate them or embarrass them; it just seems to come naturally. I would not allow MTV and other music channels to be played on my television. It was not because I dislike music. I love music that worships and honors God. It was because in my opinion there was too much graphic violence, too much sensuality and sexual innuendo, and too much foul and indecent language. I still will not allow it on my television and probably never will.

We need to take a stand for what we believe in and not back down or back off. Here is what I believe in and will stand for:

- I believe in God and His son Jesus Christ and the Holy Spirit.
- I believe God's Word is just that and completely infallible.

- I believe in the gifts of the Holy Spirit, healing and miracles.
- I believe in family.
- I believe abortion is murder unless it is to protect the life of the innocent.
- I believe euthanasia is murder too. God gives and should take life.
- I believe in America.
- I believe America was founded as, and is today, a Christian nation.
- I believe that freedom and liberty are worth dying for.
- I believe most policeman and fireman are real heroes.
- I believe our troops in and out of uniform are also heroes.
- I believe in truth, honesty and the American way.

And, I will die with those same beliefs intact. I will never recant or take back what I just said. And, you can take that to the bank!

Stepping Out

"He who kneels the most stands best." ~ D. L. Moody

Joshua 24:15 And if it seem evil unto you to serve the LORD, choose you this day whom ye will serve; whether the gods which your fathers served that were on the other side of the flood, or the gods of the Amorites, in whose land ye dwell: but as for me and my house, we will serve the LORD.

I think we need to stop worrying about what others think of us as people, or as a nation. We need to focus a little higher and worry about what God Almighty thinks of us. If I see someone in trouble, I am going to stop and help them all I can. We need to help people help themselves as much as we can. There is an old adage about giving a man a fish or teaching him how to fish that is appropriate here.

We can and should train our young people how to evangelize others, how to properly portray the Gospel of Jesus Christ, how to pray for the sick, how to cleanse lepers, how to deliver the bound and how to raise the dead. If not us, whom? If not now, when? Jesus gave us a mandate:

Matthew 10:7 And as ye go, preach, saying, The kingdom of heaven is at hand. 8 Heal the sick, cleanse the lepers, raise the dead, cast out devils: freely ye have received, freely give.

That is the mission of the Full Gospel Business Men's Fellowship International – they are God's instrument to awaken laymen, the sleeping giant of evangelism! Our mandate from God is to awaken layman to become harvest workers for Jesus Christ. In order to do that, we need to get them on fire for God by ensuring they are baptized with the Holy Spirit. Jesus said we needed His power:

Acts 1:8 But ye shall receive power, after that the Holy Ghost is come upon you: and ye shall be witnesses unto me both in

Jerusalem, and in all Judaea, and in Samaria, and unto the uttermost part of the earth.

When I was elected as the president of our local Full Gospel Business Men's Fellowship International chapter I was really surprised by it. I was not seeking the position and had given no thought to it. The men asked me if I would serve if I was elected, and I said I would. I was the busiest person I knew at the time as we had four little children in the house, I was working full time, pursuing a master's degree and serving in ministry two nights a week at the county jail. In my mind, I was the least likely candidate due to my schedule.

But God! After the election, I sat and thought about it and what the future might hold. I knew this had to be God at work so I asked Him for wisdom and guidance as I had no idea of what to do or where to go from there. In a few days, I received the following two scriptures:

Esther 4:14 For if thou altogether holdest thy peace at this time, then shall there enlargement and deliverance arise to the Jews from another place; but thou and thy father's house shall be destroyed: and <u>who knoweth whether thou art come to the kingdom for such a time as this?</u> (emphasis mine)

Daniel 11:32 And such as do wickedly against the covenant shall he corrupt by flatteries: <u>but the people that do know their God shall be strong, and do exploits.</u> (emphasis mine)

These verses, specifically the parts where I applied emphases, set the stage for my initial focus as the chapter president and I brought them to the membership for their edification too. God was telling us we were called and chosen for a time such as this, and that those who know Him will be strong and do exploits! Hallelujah! Praise God!

That is exactly where we were at the time and was exactly what we needed to hear! We do know God, and we have seen great and mighty miracles from His hand. I sense the nearness of the end of all things in this world so tangibly that I can almost taste it. If not us, then who? If not now, then when?

When we are not sure which road to take or what activity is best, then we need to ask. God will answer us and lead us, if we seek Him. He is a good, faithful and loving Father. He loves us more than we can imagine and He will always answer our honest and heartfelt questions.

If you know God has called you, but you are not sure for what purposes, then get alone with Him and ask Him to reveal it to you. He will usually give us only one step at a time. I often asked and expected Him to tell me the whole story, and was disappointed when He did not. I am not sure why I did that. Maybe I wanted the right to approve it or not, but He is God and I am not. If I knew it all, and it was ugly or scary, I might balk and mess the whole thing up.

God will give us the next step. Our obligation is to obey that and step out immediately. Anything less is disobedience and will stop the flow until we obey the last thing we heard.

Rules for the Road

"Your mind does not stay renewed anymore than your hair stays combed." ~ Kenneth Hagin

The book of Romans, chapter 12 contains instructions for the church. I want to walk thru this chapter and discuss how a warrior would use it as a guide to life.

Romans 12:1 I beseech you therefore, brethren, by the mercies of God, that ye present your bodies a living sacrifice, holy, acceptable unto God, *which is* your reasonable service.

Our reasonable service is to surrender all to God. He made us, and sustains us and is helping us become what He intended us to be from the very beginning. We should offer ourselves to Him completely. Isaiah 6 verse 8 talks about this

Isaiah 6:8 Also I heard the voice of the Lord, saying, Whom shall I send, and who will go for us? Then said I, Here *am* I; send me.

Be careful when you pray that prayer! God will honor it and you will be challenged. But, in a very good way!

Romans 12:2 And be not conformed to this world: but be ye transformed by the renewing of your mind, that ye may prove what *is* that good, and acceptable, and perfect, will of God.

How do we renew our minds? We renew our minds by being immersed into the living Word of God and praying in tongues. We need to read the Word every single day, and if we do, we will grow to know God as He reveals Himself to us through His Word via revelation by the Holy Spirit. And, we will learn and understand what God's perfect will for us is so we can walk in it.

If we do not renew our minds by this continual washing of the Word, we will become weaker spiritually and remain deceived by the enemy. This is so critical to our growth.

Romans 12:3 For I say, through the grace given unto me, to every man that is among you, not to think *of himself* more highly than he ought to think; but to think soberly, according as God hath dealt to every man the measure of faith.

We always need to remember that without Jesus we can do no good thing. Whatever we have or whatever we are good at is because of Him. We need to remain humble and not grow proud over the gifts and graces we receive from the Holy Spirit.

Romans 12:4 For as we have many members in one body, and all members have not the same office: 5 So we, *being* many, are one body in Christ, and every one members one of another.

We are dependent on one another and fit together by the Lord into the body of Christ. Maybe not in the way we may think or want but as the body needs us and as the Lord created and empowers us.

Romans 12:6 Having then gifts differing according to the grace that is given to us, whether prophecy, *let us prophesy* according to the proportion of faith; 7 Or ministry, *let us wait* on *our* ministering: or he that teacheth, on teaching; 8 Or he that exhorteth, on exhortation: he that giveth, *let him do it* with simplicity; he that ruleth, with diligence; he that sheweth mercy, with cheerfulness.

Whatever our gift is, let us be diligent about it and remain faithful and true in offering that gift to the body of Christ. We are endowed so we might serve others with whatever it is that we are gifted with. These gifts are not intended for our own personal private gain but are intended for the body at large.

Romans 12:9 *Let* love be without dissimulation. Abhor that which is evil; cleave to that which is good.

We must not let our love grow cold or become hypocrisy and we must live above reproach without any appearance of evil. We are told to abhor or hate evil and cleave or cling to all that is good. From this point on, we begin to target each individual Christian with the instructions that follow.

Romans 12:10 *Be* kindly affectioned one to another with brotherly love; in honour preferring one another;

This is speaking of brotherly love and honoring one another for those that are in Christ Jesus. We should have a genuine and heartfelt love for the body of Christians and feel a real kinship with those who walk in Him.

Romans 12:11 Not slothful in business; fervent in spirit; serving the Lord;

We should be diligent about our business, or our working lives too and not lazy or putting things off for another day. Being fervent means being hot and enthusiastic and not being cool to the spirit as we serve the Lord.

Romans 12:12 Rejoicing in hope; patient in tribulation; continuing instant in prayer;

Our lives should be always hopeful and rejoicing. We need to be patient when enduring trials and tribulations as we understand that they are for our spiritual growth. Instant in prayer speaks of being in a state of prayer and communication with God at all times.

Romans 12:13 Distributing to the necessity of saints; given to hospitality.

We should be ready to assist the body of Christ at all times with all of our means that are at our disposal, and we should be hospitable and willing to feed, clothe and shelter those sent to us.

Romans 12:14 Bless them which persecute you: bless, and curse not.

We are expressly told not to curse those who persecute us. We are to bless them instead, no matter how hard this may be. It will take some effort in the beginning, but will get easier as time goes on. Jesus prayed the mercy prayer for those who crucified him, "Father, forgive them because they do not understand what they are doing." We should be willing to do likewise.

Romans 12:15 Rejoice with them that do rejoice, and weep with them that weep.

Life is indeed about people and we need to be sensitive to the needs of those around us. You do not sing to someone who is in mourning nor do we put a damper on joyous occasions. Be real and be involved with all you encounter. Remember, it is our actions that sway others – more than our words.

Romans 12:16 *Be* of the same mind one toward another. Mind not high things, but condescend to men of low estate. Be not wise in your own conceits.

We must not be proud or conceited about ourselves, our ministries or our knowledge of the Holy One. We should never think we are it! The adage I hear in my mind when I think of this verse is "but for the grace of God, there go I." I am no better than any of my brothers and I need to remember my roots, or where I came from.

Romans 12:17 Recompense to no man evil for evil. Provide things honest in the sight of all men.

We do not fight evil with evil. There can never ever be a time when doing wrong is right. So, no matter how hard it may be, we must answer evil with good – in every situation.

Romans 12:18 If it be possible, as much as lieth in you, live peaceably with all men.

We should be known as peacemakers and not peace takers. According to the book of Proverbs, contention comes from pride and if we leave it alone all strife and reproach will stop. We are told not to argue over the finer points of the law, or scripture but to give each other grace since none of us knows it all. We are to contend for the faith, but in a peaceable and friendly way.

Romans 12:19 Dearly beloved, avenge not yourselves, but *rather* give place unto wrath: for it is written, Vengeance *is* mine; I will repay, saith the Lord.

The Lord tells us "vengeance is mine sayeth the Lord" so we will not be deceived into thinking that we can take matters into our own hands and render justice or judgment to another. Only God knows the heart and intentions of a man's heart and only He can render absolute justice.

Romans 12:20 Therefore if thine enemy hunger, feed him; if he thirst, give him drink: for in so doing thou shalt heap coals of fire on his head.

How do we treat an enemy? We should feed, clothe and care for him and his needs. After all, he is made in the image of God too and Jesus went to the cross for him as well as He did for me. The scripture states that when we do this, we actually pile recompense upon his head and the Lord who is perfect in all His ways will execute judgment.

Romans 12:21 Be not overcome of evil, but overcome evil with good.

Finally, the only way to fight evil is with good. We actually overcome evil when we answer it with good!

Wait upon the Lord

"Fulfillment of your destiny does not come in a moment, a month, or a year, but over a lifetime." ~ Casey Treat

Saul was impetuous and he did not understand how to follow God. He made mistake after mistake, but one of the greatest mistakes he made was failing to wait upon the Lord. His enemy, the Philistines had gathered and were arrayed against him in great numbers so that he was heavily outnumbered. Samuel sent him to Gilgal and told him to wait there until he arrived.

1 Samuel 13:8 And he tarried seven days, according to the set time that Samuel had appointed: but Samuel came not to Gilgal; and the people were scattered from him.

Saul was afraid because the people were drifting away, hiding and leaving his ranks while he waited on Samuel to show up. So, he took matters in his own hands and offered a sacrifice unto the Lord without Samuel. He was not anointed as a priest, but as king so he had no business offering a sacrifice at all. Secondly, he was moved by fear of man, fear of the enemy and his own fears to act when he should have sought the Lord. In all fairness, Saul probably thought he was seeking the Lord. But, fear is the opposite of faith, and only faith pleases God.

1 Samuel 13:11-12 And Samuel said, What hast thou done? And Saul said, Because I saw that the people were scattered from me, and that thou camest not within the days appointed, and that the Philistines gathered themselves together at Michmash; 12 Therefore said I, The Philistines will come down now upon me to Gilgal, and I have not made supplication unto the LORD: I forced myself therefore, and offered a burnt offering.

Saul lost it all due to his inability to wait for Samuel and obey the prophet. There are going to be times when it is hard to know when to move and when to act, and when to wait upon the Lord. One thing is absolutely certain. We do not want to proceed until we hear from God because if God is not in it, we do not want any part of it either. But, here are some guidelines:

- We are to wait
- He is God
- He forms, builds, causes, works, does, teaches, leads and inspires

Psalms 25:3 Yea, let none that wait on thee be ashamed: let them be ashamed which transgress without cause.

We transgress when we become impatient or lose our trust in God.

Psalms 25:5 Lead me in thy truth, and teach me: for thou *art* the God of my salvation; on thee do I wait all the day.

How long should we wait? All day if necessary! We are waiting to be lead and to be taught.

Psalms 37:7 Rest in the LORD, and wait patiently for him: fret not thyself because of him who prospereth in his way, because of the man who bringeth wicked devices to pass.

Waiting and resting go hand in hand. If we are waiting, we should be at peace knowing that God will show us the way He wants us to go. If we are at peace, we can rest and gather our strength.

Psalms 62:5 My soul, wait thou only upon God; for my expectation *is* from him. 6 He only *is* my rock and my salvation: *he is* my defense; I shall not be moved. 7 In God *is* my salvation and my glory: the rock of my strength, *and* my refuge, *is* in God.

All we need comes from God so we do not need to be busy or fretful or wondering when it will arrive. He provides everything we need before the need arises. Waiting entails confident expectation in what God will do.

Psalms 46:10 Be still, and know that I *am* God: I will be exalted among the heathen, I will be exalted in the earth.

Psalms 130:5 I wait for the LORD, my soul doth wait, and in his word do I hope. 6 My soul *waiteth* for the Lord more than they that watch for the morning: *I say, more than* they that watch for the morning.

So, we wait. We rest and hope for what God is going to do to lead us in the direction he wants us to go. We are not idle but fully engaged, expecting God to show us His way. We pray and ask for guidance, for His wisdom in the situation or issue or problem. Then, we wait for Him to answer. He will not fail us, but we need to wait until He does answer.

Remember, he is Lord. He is sovereign and knew the end from the beginning. He may answer immediately or relatively soon or it may take a while. In any case, once we ask and place it with Him, the only right thing to do is to wait until He shows us what to do. Anything less negates our hope, our trust and our faith.

What's Next?

"Preach the gospel every day; if necessary, use words." ~ St Francis of Assisi

"If you have men who will only come if they know there is a good road, I do not want them. I want men who will come if there is no road at all." ~ David Livingstone

Micah 3:8 But truly I am full of power by the spirit of the LORD, and of judgment, and of might, to declare unto Jacob his transgression, and to Israel his sin.

Ezekiel 3:8 Behold, I have made thy face strong against their faces, and thy forehead strong against their foreheads.

"Live so as to be missed when dead." ~ Robert Murray McCheyne

What's Next?

Here are some facts[1] I have seen posted recently:

- In the past ten years some 37,000 American churches have closed their doors.
- Churches in the U.S. lose about 2,765,000 members each year as "drop-outs."
- For various reasons, 18,000 pastors leave the ministry annually.
- Only 2.2% of churches in the United States are growing by conversion-increase.

I honestly think we are seeing the beginning of the end of the denominational age of Christianity in America. We are going back to an identity with Jesus rather than an identity with a particular denomination. Many of the old main line churches are aging themselves right out of existence. I recently attended a church service where there was no one in the sanctuary under the age of 65. Then, another and another.

Mainline Protestant denominations continue to decline,[2] according to the 2006 Yearbook of American and Canadian Churches. The United Methodist Church, the Evangelical Lutheran Church in America, the Presbyterian Church USA, and the United Church of Christ, all reported decreases in membership in 2005.

I heard a statistic that only 4% of the next generation will be involved in Evangelical Christianity.[3] To evangelize means you explain your beliefs to others with the view that they might want to adopt your beliefs. An evangelist is someone who preaches the Gospel to try to get people saved and on their way to Heaven. The English words come from Greek words that mean to announce good news, bring a good message, or preach the Gospel.

By God's own hand, the church in America is entering a period where denominationalism is falling away. As hard as it may be to believe, at a recent annual meeting of the Southern Baptist Convention (SBC), the anticipated growth-statistic showed that the

SBC will be gone in just five generations. The Church of England in recent years permanently closed more than 600 churches.

The church as we know it is rapidly changing. America is changing very quickly too. The America I grew up in does not exist any longer. Time is coming to a close. We need to be about the work of calling men out of the world so we can perform the work needed to bring in the last great harvest. We need to separate ourselves from this world, from the lusts of the flesh, the lust of the eyes and the pride of life.

1 John 2:16 For all that is in the world, the lust of the flesh, and the lust of the eyes, and the pride of life, is not of the Father, but is of the world.

I recently saw a statistic where there is no known single Christian leader in this country: A new Barna Group study[4] asked people to identify the single most influential Christian leader in the U.S. today. 41% were unable to think of anyone who would meet that description. Billy Graham was mentioned by 19%, 9% named the Pope, and 8% President Barack Obama. 5% identified Joel Osteen, 2% Charles Stanley, and 2% Joyce Meyer.

But, ask football fans about a man named Tebow! Ridiculed, maligned and criticized by nearly every sportscaster in the country, Tim Tebow still comes across as an honest, humble, considerate and generous man who is a good football player in spite of all the negative reviews. There were millions of conversations concerning Denver quarterback Tim Tebow and the "prophetic" statistics that accompanied his football game on January 8, 2012.[5] The connection between John 3:16 (which is Tim Tebow's favorite verse) with his 316 passing yards and 31.6 gain completion average has stimulated the spiritual awareness of the nation.

God is still raising up those whom he wants to raise up without regard to what men might think! Tim Tebow has captured the imagination of American Football fans and has refused to yield or compromise on his convictions. He is a true spiritual warrior and I am very proud of him. We need more leaders in our country and around the world who are like that!

We need to find, select and train the leaders who will lead us into the last great revival! We need new Christian leadership that will not compromise with sin or evil. We need leaders that will not be afraid to rock the boat and who are not primarily concerned with being politically correct. We need leaders who will not back down in the face of criticism, ridicule or persecution. That is the call on my life, and I hope you will make it the call on your lives as well.

The next step after awakening laymen is to teach them how to discern the activities of the enemy, and then to seek him out and destroy his works. Those are the titles of the next two volumes of this series, *Volume 2 – Discerning Enemy Activity* and *Volume 3 – Destroying the Enemy's Works*. I hope you will continue with me on this journey of discovery to find and activate valiant warriors for our Lord and savior Jesus, the Anointed One!

May the Lord of all creation bless you with great favor, great peace, great courage and great wisdom as you seek His will for your life. May He bless you with health, light, life and great vision. May the Lord hold you and your loved ones close and give you rest. In the name of Jesus, the Anointed One I pray. Amen and amen.

Appendixes

Appendix A – The Vision

In the middle of the night as Demos prayed kneeling on the carpet in his living room, he received a vision.

"The Vision" as told by Demos Shakarian (1952)

"My son, I knew you before you were born. I have guided you every step of the way. Now I am going to show you the purpose of your life."

Although I remained on my knees, I felt as if I were rising and moving up, away from the living room. Down below me I could see the rooftops of Downey. There were the San Bernardino Mountains, and over there the coast of the Pacific. Now I was high above the earth, able to see the entire country from west to east. Although I could see so far, I could also see people on the earth – millions and millions of people standing shoulder to shoulder. Then, just as a camera can zoom in at a football game to show first the stadium, then the players, and then the very laces on the football, my vision seemed to move in on these millions. I could see tiny details of thousands and thousands of faces.

And what I saw terrified me. The faces were set, lifeless, and miserable. Though the people stood so close together, shoulders touching, there was no real contact between them. They stared straight ahead, unblinking, unseeing. What a shudder of horror, I realized that they were dead…

The vision changed. Whether the world was turning, or whether I was traveling around it, I did not know. But now beneath me was the continent of South America. Then on to Africa, Europe, Asia. Once more the startling close-ups occurred, and everywhere it was the same. Brown faces, black faces – every one rigid, wretched, each locked in his own private death.

"Lord!" I cried, "What is the matter with them! Lord, help them!"

"My son, what you see next is going to happen very soon."

The earth was turning – or I was moving around it – a second time. Below me again were millions upon millions of men. But what a difference! This time heads were raised. Eyes shone with joy. Hands were lifted towards heaven. These who had been so isolated, each in his prison of self, were linked in a community of love and adoration. Asia, Africa, America – everywhere – death had turned to life.

And the Vision was over. I felt myself returning to my living room…

Demos Shakarian

Appendix B – Daily Affirmations

- I am an object of God's love, nothing can separate me from that love (Romans 8:39).
- I am a child of God (John 1:12; Romans 8:16).
- Jesus Christ is my Lord, Savior, and friend (1 Corinthians 12:3; John 15:15).
- I am born again of the Spirit (John 3:3,7; 1 Peter 1:23).
- I am a new creation; old things have passed away (2 Corinthians 5:17).
- I am saved by His grace, through faith (Ephesians 2:8-9).
- I have an immutable covenant with the Creator, sworn by Himself (Hebrews 6:13-20).
- That covenant was ratified in His own blood (Mark 14:24).
- I am blessed (Psalm 1:1).
- I am Abraham's seed (2 Corinthians 11:22).
- I have the blessing of Abraham (Galatians 3:14).
- I am blessed with every spiritual blessing in heavenly places in Christ (Ephesians 1:3).
- My wife of noble character is my crown (Proverbs 12:4, NIV).
- My children are blessed (Proverbs 20:7).
- My descendants will be mighty on the earth (Psalm 112:2).
- I have an abundant life (John 10:10).
- God has filled and empowered me with His Spirit (Acts 1:8).
- I was chosen in Him before the foundation of the world (Ephesians 1:4).
- God predestined me, called me, justified me, and will glorify me (Romans 8:30).
- All my sins are forgiven (Psalm 103:3a).
- He heals all my diseases (Psalm 103:3b, Matthew 8:17, 1 Peter 2:24).
- He causes me to prosper and be in health (Proverbs 10:22; 3 John 2).

- I am rich (2 Corinthians 8:9).
- I can do all things through Christ who strengthens me (Philippians 4:13).
- I am a joint heir with Jesus Christ (Romans 8:17).
- It was the Father's good pleasure to give me the kingdom (Luke 12:32).
- If I believe it, speak it, and do not doubt it, I can move mountains (Mark 11:23).
- Things I pray for, if I believe I receive them, I shall have them (Mark 11:24).
- As He is, so am I in this world (1 John 4:17).
- He supplies all my needs according to His riches in glory (Philippians 4:19).
- No evil shall come upon me, nor shall any sickness come near my house (Psalm 91:10).
- He gives His angels charge over me (Psalm 91:11).
- An angel encamps all around me (Psalm 34:7).
- I am strong in the Lord and in the power of His might (Ephesians 6:10).
- He has given me authority over all the power of Satan (Luke 10:19).
- Nothing Satan does can hurt me (Luke 10:19).
- I cast out demons (Mark 16:17).
- I lay hands on the sick and they shall recover (Mark 16:18).
- God causes all things to work together for my good (Romans 8:28).
- Christ is my wisdom, righteousness, sanctification, and redemption (1 Corinthians 1:30).
- He is my peace (Ephesians 2:14).
- I fear no evil, for He is with me (Psalm 23:4).
- I am not afraid of evil reports; my heart is steadfast, trusting in the Lord (Psalm 112:7).
- Jesus has gone to prepare a place for me (John 14:2).
- Eye has not seen nor ear heard what God has prepared for me (1 Corinthians 2:9).

Appendix B – Daily Affirmations

- He will satisfy me with long life (Psalm 91:16).
- Goodness and mercy shall follow me all the days of my life (Psalm 23:6).
- When I leave my body, I will be present with the Lord, forever (2 Corinthians 5:8).
- If He returns before I die, I will meet Him in the air, maybe soon (1 Thessalonians 4:17).

Appendix C – Impartation of the Warrior Anointing

Dear heavenly Father, in the name of Jesus I ask you to come precious Holy Spirit and settle on me right now. Rest on me in all your fullness and glory. In the name of Jesus, I receive the impartation of the Warrior Anointing of God Most High.

This anointing is a breaker anointing that will empower me to live above the snake line and to walk in dunamis power as I walk in the Spirit. This anointing will cause the enemy and his forces to flee from the mighty power of God that rests on me. The enemies forces cannot stand against me as I walk in divine favor in every aspect of my life. I walk in divine protection and am guarded at all times by mighty warring angels.

I am empowered with great faith, great peace, great love, a sound mind, a kind and gentle spirit, great self control, great generosity and great wisdom in all matters pertaining to the advancement of the kingdom of God. I walk in the favor of the Most High.

Father, bless me now with your presence, your glory and your power to do all You created me to do in the matchless name of Jesus, the Anointed One!

Amen and amen

Appendix D - Roman Road to Salvation

Romans 3:10 As it is written, There is none righteous, no, not one:

Romans 3:23 For all have sinned, and come short of the glory of God;

Romans 5:8 But God commendeth his love toward us, in that, while we were yet sinners, Christ died for us.

Romans 6:23 For the wages of sin is death; but the gift of God is eternal life through Jesus Christ our Lord.

Romans 10:13 For whosoever shall call upon the name of the Lord shall be saved.

Romans 10:9-10 That if thou shalt confess with thy mouth the Lord Jesus, and shalt believe in thine heart that God hath raised him from the dead, thou shalt be saved. 10 For with the heart man believeth unto righteousness; and with the mouth confession is made unto salvation.

If you believe that Jesus Christ is the son of God, that He came and lived as a man and was crucified and put to death for your sins and mine; and that He was raised back to life three days later, then pray this prayer aloud to become born again:

Father God, I confess I am a sinner and I ask you to forgive me of my sins. I believe that Jesus is your son and that he came and lived and died to pay my penalty for my sins. I thank you for His work on my behalf. I believe Jesus was raised back to life and now sits at Your right hand preparing to return and gather His people. I ask You to come into my heart and help me to live as You would have me to live. In Jesus' name I pray. Amen

Appendix E - Recommended Reading

- *4 Keys to Hearing God's Voice*, by Mark and Patti Virkler
- *developing a Supernatural Lifestyle, a Practical Guide*, by Kris Vallotton
- *living the SPIRIT FORMED LIFE*, by Jack Hayford
- *Man of Valor*, by Richard Exley
- *The Blessing of the Lord Makes Rich and He Adds No Sorrow With It*, by Kenneth Copeland
- *The Blood and the Glory*, by Billye Brim
- *The Bondage Breaker*, by Neil T. Anderson
- *The Spiritual Warrior's Prayer Guide,* by Quin Sherrer and Ruthanne Garlock
- *The Three Battlefields*, by Francis Frangipane
- *The Walk of the Spirit – The Walk of Power,* by Dave Roberson
- *The Way of the Warrior Series*, by Graham Cooke
- *Qualities of a Spiritual Warrior*, by Graham Cooke
- *Manifesting Your Spirit*, by Graham Cooke
- *The Way of the Warrior*, by Harry R. Jackson Jr
- *This Day We Fight*, by Francis Frangipane
- *Time to Defeat the Devil*, by Chuck Pierce

End notes

A Call to Arms

1. Cassie Bernall, Columbine High Martyr – there is some controversy whether or not Cassie Bernall ever uttered these words before she was viciously murdered. However, I am absolutely convinced this was her confession as this is also another marker, or sign of where we are on the Lord's clock. Those who oppose this are also against anything that speaks of righteousness or godliness.

2. 2011 Tōhoku earthquake and tsunami, From Wikipedia, the free encyclopedia.

3. Tucson Shooting, Chicago Tribune, A Year in Review.

4. Haiti Earthquake - Massachusetts officials seek to keep focus on Haiti, 2 years after devastating earthquake. Posted on Breaking News - MassLive.com on January 30, 2012, 5:37 PM.

5. Virginia Tech massacre, From Wikipedia, the free encyclopedia.

6. 2004 Indian Ocean earthquake and tsunami, From Wikipedia, the free encyclopedia.

7. Columbine High School massacre, from Wikipedia, the free encyclopedia.

8. The number of pregnancies and birth data source is the National Vital Statistics System, of the Centers for Disease Control from their final 2009 calculations. The primary statistics are as follows:

Birth Data for United States in 2009
Number of births: 4,130,665
Birth rate: 13.5 per 1,000 population
Fertility rate: 66.7 births per 1000 women aged 15-44 years
Percent born low birthweight: 8.2%
Percent unmarried: 41.0%

Studies estimating the incidence of prenatal alcohol and drug exposure:

Alcohol: 2.6 million infants each year are prenatally exposed to alcohol (Gomby and Shiono, 1991).

Illicit Drugs: Each year, 11% of all newborns, or 459,690, are exposed to illicit drugs (Chasnoff, 1989).

More than 739,000 women each year use one or more illicit drugs during pregnancy (Gomby and Shiono, 1991).

9. The Golden Chain refers to a strategy Demos Shakarian put forth where one spirit-filled believer brought a friend, a neighbor or family member to Jesus, who then would do the same thing – bring another friend, neighbor or family member to Jesus, and so on and so on. Continuing until the whole world was reached with the gospel of Jesus Christ.

Dunamis Power

1. Hebrew thinking is doing and dynamic, vigorous, passionate, and sometimes quite explosive in kind; correspondingly Greek thinking is knowing and static [harmonic or resting], peaceful, moderate.

Keys to Success

1. Father's Love Letter - A paraphrased compilation of Bible verses that are presented in the form of a love letter from God. Available in various multimedia formats and languages from Barry Adams.

2. The Spokane Chronicle, Saturday, March 23, 1918.

3. National Public Radio, Penn State Abuse Scandal: A Guide And Timeline, by Bill Chappell, January 8, 2012.

4. 1900-2000: A century of genocides, by Piero Scaruffi.

End Notes

5. The Right Scoop, SHOCK – Brain surgeon confirms ObamaCare rations care, has death panels! on November 23rd, 2011 in Politics.

6. Unit 731, From Wikipedia, the free encyclopedia.

What's Next?

1. Charles Carrin Ministries, I DON'T WANT TO SCARE YOU —SO PLEASE READ TO THE END! Posted by Charles Carrin on Tuesday, May 31, 2011; Originally published in March 2011.

2. USA Today, Growth stalls, falls for largest U.S. churches, By Richard Yeakley, Religion News Service; Updated 2/15/2011 6:44:10 PM.

3. Sid Roth, It's Supernatural, Rebecca Greenwood. January 16, 2012.

4. Barna Group, U.S. Lacks Notable Christian Leaders, November 21, 2011.

5. Protestant Reforming: The Reformation of a Protestant Mind, Tim Tebow & Tebowmania, blog entry; and Francis Frangipane's web site.

Glossary

Agape Love – The Greek word agape is often translated "love" in the New Testament. Agape love is different from other types of love in that it is essence is self-sacrifice. Unlike our English word love, agape is not used in the Bible to refer to romantic or sexual love. Nor does it refer to close friendship or brotherly love, for which the Greek word philia is used. Nor does agape mean charity, a term which the King James translators carried over from the Latin. Agape love is unique and is distinguished by its nature and character. Agape is love which is of and from God, whose very nature is love itself.

Anointing – The Spirit of the Lord, the Anointing, the Holy Ghost and Power are all synonymous terms. Simply put, the anointing is God's power. It is the manifestation and the result of his presence.

Belial – Belial is derived by some from beli, not, and âl, over, i.e., one so proud and envious as not to bear a superior; by others, from beli, not, and ol, a yoke, i.e., a lawless, ungovernable person, andres paranomoi, "lawless men," as the LXX render. It is, however, more probably derived from beli, not, and yäâl, profit, i.e., a worthless person, good for nothing to himself or others, and capable of nothing but mischief.

Besetting Sins – Beset means: 1. To attack from all sides. 2. To trouble persistently; harass. 3. To hem in; surround: "the mountains which beset it round." (Nathaniel Hawthorne).

Born Again – see Saved.

Breaker Anointing – Micah 2:13 - The one who breaks open will come up before them; they will break out, pass through the gate, and go out by it; their king will pass before them, with the Lord at their head.

What does it take for heaven to invade earth? It takes a breaker

Glossary

anointing! One of God's names in the Bible actually is the "Breaker." A breaker anointing is a catalytic deposit of the Holy Spirit where eternity breaks through into the natural realm. It is a holy invasion where the gates of heaven are opened!

This type of anointing breaks through every obstacle and hindrance to the furtherance of the Gospel. It shakes every shackle loose that holds individuals and the Church back from coming into their destiny and inheritance. Jesus promises that "the Kingdom suffers violence and the violent take it by force." The breaker anointing is the core anointing of the apostolic church for advancement.

Cessationist – In Christian theology, Cessationism is the view that the miraculous gifts of the Holy Spirit, such as tongues, prophecy and healing, ceased being practiced early on in Church history. Cessationists generally believe that the miraculous gifts were given only for the foundation of the Church, during the time between the coming of the Holy Spirit on Pentecost, c. AD 33 (see Acts 2) and the fulfillment of God's purposes in history, usually identified as either the completion of the last book of the New Testament or the death of the last Apostle, i.e. John the Apostle.

Evangelical Christianity – The National Association of Evangelicals defines an evangelical as someone: who believes that the Bible is authoritative, who has had a born-again experience and who shares this message of faith.

Favor – friendly or kind regard; good will; approval; liking; unfair partiality; favoritism; attractiveness; to be partial to; prefer; to help; assist; to do a kindness for; endorsing. To be favored means: regarded or treated with favor; provided with advantages; especially privileged.

Golden Chain of Men – refers to a vision Demos Shakarian had where men would learn of Jesus, then work to save their family, and then train other men to do the same thing.

Impartation – is the imparting of some spiritual gift from one spirit-filled believer to another. This is accomplished by prayer and may involve the laying on of hands.

Koinoinia – is a Greek word that occurs 20 times in the Bible. Koinonia's primary meaning is fellowship, sharing in common, communion; that means communion by intimate participation.

Layman – a person who is not a member of the clergy; one of the laity. a person who is not a member of a given profession, as law or medicine. Layman, "laity": in short: means common people.

Philia love – means friendship or affectionate love in modern Greek. It is a dispassionate virtuous love, a concept developed by Aristotle. It includes loyalty to friends, family, and community, and requires virtue, equality and familiarity. In ancient texts, philos denoted a general type of love, used for love between family, between friends, a desire or enjoyment of an activity, as well as between lovers.

Saved – is that state of a person where they have invited Jesus to be their Lord, Master and Savior and to come into their hearts and reign. This is the state of a person that knows that they belong to God and cannot be pried out of His grasp. "They know that they know" is how I have often heard this expressed.

School of the Spirit – there are many fine organizations who are actively running schools of the Spirit for students. Many are affiliated with the Quakers and Franciscans, but that is not what I am referring to in this book. My reference is to the active leading, teaching and training of the Holy Spirit in my life. For well over fifteen years now, the precious Holy Spirit has been leading me from one spiritual discipline to another, from one book to another, from one teaching to another. I have felt His hand upon me, and His leading in so many areas. It truly is a marvel to me that he would spend so much time and effort on me. If this hasn't been your experience, pray for this. It is wonderful to say the least as He is the very best teacher in the entire world.

Snake Line – is a concept I heard from Jesse Duplantis that talks about where the devil is actively working in our lives to cause us to stumble and fall, either by or into sin. While we are down there in it, it is hard to see. Once we rise above it, we can see his ways and wiles more clearly.

Warrior Anointing – is to open doors, to lead the way to show people they can be more than they thought they could be. It gives people permission to dream large and to experience God for themselves in ways unheard of in traditional denominational churches. It presents a manner of fellowship, encouragement, development and opportunity to equip and prepare people for a powerful life of destiny. It releases people to find their inheritance, to live and walk in the favor of the Most High, to live and give out of abundance and blessing in such a way that it will transform the world around them.

The idea of an anointed warrior was originally taught and promoted by John and Carol Arnott, pastors of the Toronto Christian Fellowship. The Warrior Anointing was introduced after Carol Arnott prophesied about a "Golden Sword." The anointing is said to bring deliverance from your enemies and was most popular among adherents of the Toronto Blessing Movement.

About the Author

Mr. Alan Barrett Keyte is a spirit-filled, ordained minister of the Gospel who is on fire for Jesus. He is an author, counselor, evangelist and teacher currently serving as the President of the Tucson, Arizona chapter of the Full Gospel Business Men's Fellowship International.

He is finishing up a master's degree in Clinical Pastoral Counseling at Colorado Theological Seminary. Alan is a graduate of Francis Frangipane's, *In Christ's Image Training*; both phase I and phase II. Mr. Keyte has also completed Global Awakening's *Healing School 1* and *Healing School 2*.

Alan is very active in local ministries especially in jail and prison ministry, and teaches Experiencing God, the Seven Steps to Freedom and How to Hear God courses. He is the principle counselor at Living Waters Christian Counseling, and volunteers at the Pima County Jail, local hospitals and as a Chaplain with the Billy Graham Evangelistic Association's, Rapid Response Team.

Alan and his wife Peggy reside on a small ranch northwest of Tucson, Arizona and have a very large and growing family with seven children, six grandchildren and four great grandchildren.

Made in the USA
Charleston, SC
11 August 2012